TO THE LIGHTHOUSE

Virginia Woolf

EDITORIAL DIRECTOR Laurie Barnett
DIRECTOR OF TECHNOLOGY Tammy Hepps

SERIES EDITOR John Crowther
MANAGING EDITOR Vincent Janoski

WRITERS David Hopson, Brian Phillips
EDITORS Jane Carr, Benjamin Morgan

This edition published by Spark Publishing

Spark Publishing
A Division of SparkNotes LLC
120 Fifth Avenue, 8th Floor
New York, NY 10011

Please submit all comments and questions or report errors to www.sparknotes.com/errors

Printed and bound in the United States

ISBN 1-58663-493-3

INTRODUCTION: STOPPING TO BUY SPARKNOTES ON A SNOWY EVENING

Whose words these are you *think* you know.
Your paper's due tomorrow, though;
We're glad to see you stopping here
To get some help before you go.

Lost your course? You'll find it here.
Face tests and essays without fear.
Between the words, good grades at stake:
Get great results throughout the year.

Once school bells caused your heart to quake
As teachers circled each mistake.
Use SparkNotes and no longer weep,
Ace every single test you take.

Yes, books are lovely, dark, and deep,
But only what you grasp you keep,
With hours to go before you sleep,
With hours to go before you sleep.

Contents

CONTEXT   1

PLOT OVERVIEW   3

CHARACTER LIST   5

ANALYSIS OF MAJOR CHARACTERS   9
    MRS. RAMSAY   9
    MR. RAMSAY   10
    LILY BRISCOE   10
    JAMES RAMSAY   11

THEMES, MOTIFS & SYMBOLS   13
    THE TRANSIENCE OF LIFE AND WORK   13
    ART AS A MEANS OF PRESERVATION   13
    THE SUBJECTIVE NATURE OF REALITY   14
    THE RESTORATIVE EFFECTS OF BEAUTY   14
    THE DIFFERING BEHAVIORS OF MEN AND WOMEN   15
    BRACKETS   15
    THE LIGHTHOUSE   16
    LILY'S PAINTING   16
    THE RAMSAYS' HOUSE   17
    THE SEA   17
    THE BOAR'S SKULL   17
    THE FRUIT BASKET   18

SUMMARY & ANALYSIS   19
    THE WINDOW: CHAPTERS I–IV   19
    THE WINDOW: CHAPTERS V–VIII   22
    THE WINDOW: CHAPTERS IX–XI   25
    THE WINDOW: CHAPTERS XII–XVI   28
    THE WINDOW: CHAPTER XVII   31
    THE WINDOW: CHAPTERS XVIII–XIX   34
    TIME PASSES: CHAPTERS I–X   37

THE LIGHTHOUSE: CHAPTERS I–III   40

THE LIGHTHOUSE: CHAPTERS IV–VII   43

THE LIGHTHOUSE: CHAPTERS VIII–XIII   46

IMPORTANT QUOTATIONS EXPLAINED   51

KEY FACTS   57

STUDY QUESTIONS & ESSAY TOPICS   59

REVIEW & RESOURCES   63

     QUIZ   63

     SUGGESTIONS FOR FURTHER READING   68

Context

VIRGINIA WOOLF WAS BORN on January 25, 1882, a descendant of one of Victorian England's most prestigious literary families. Her father, Sir Leslie Stephen, was the editor of the *Dictionary of National Biography* and was married to the daughter of the writer William Thackeray. Woolf grew up among the most important and influential British intellectuals of her time, and received free rein to explore her father's library. Her personal connections and abundant talent soon opened doors for her. Woolf wrote that she found herself in "a position where it was easier on the whole to be eminent than obscure." Almost from the beginning, her life was a precarious balance of extraordinary success and mental instability.

As a young woman, Woolf wrote for the prestigious *Times Literary Supplement,* and as an adult she quickly found herself at the center of England's most important literary community. Known as the "Bloomsbury Group" after the section of London in which its members lived, this group of writers, artists, and philosophers emphasized nonconformity, aesthetic pleasure, and intellectual freedom, and included such luminaries as the painter Lytton Strachey, the novelist E. M. Forster, the composer Benjamin Britten, and the economist John Maynard Keynes. Working among such an inspirational group of peers and possessing an incredible talent in her own right, Woolf published her most famous novels by the mid-1920s, including *The Voyage Out, Mrs. Dalloway, Orlando,* and *To the Lighthouse.* With these works she reached the pinnacle of her profession.

Woolf's life was equally dominated by mental illness. Her parents died when she was young—her mother in 1895 and her father in 1904—and she was prone to intense, terrible headaches and emotional breakdowns. After her father's death, she attempted suicide, throwing herself out a window. Though she married Leonard Woolf in 1912 and loved him deeply, she was not entirely satisfied romantically or sexually. For years she sustained an intimate relationship with the novelist Vita Sackville-West. Late in life, Woolf became terrified by the idea that another nervous breakdown was close at hand, one from which she would not recover. On March 28, 1941, she wrote her husband a note stating that she did not wish to spoil his life by going mad. She then drowned herself in the River Ouse.

Woolf's writing bears the mark of her literary pedigree as well as her struggle to find meaning in her own unsteady existence. Written in a poised, understated, and elegant style, her work examines the structures of human life, from the nature of relationships to the experience of time. Yet her writing also addresses issues relevant to her era and literary circle. Throughout her work she celebrates and analyzes the Bloomsbury values of aestheticism, feminism, and independence. Moreover, her stream-of-consciousness style was influenced by, and responded to, the work of the French thinker Henri Bergson and the novelists Marcel Proust and James Joyce.

This style allows the subjective mental processes of Woolf's characters to determine the objective content of her narrative. In *To the Lighthouse* (1927), one of her most experimental works, the passage of time, for example, is modulated by the consciousness of the characters rather than by the clock. The events of a single afternoon constitute over half the book, while the events of the following ten years are compressed into a few dozen pages. Many readers of *To the Lighthouse*, especially those who are not versed in the traditions of modernist fiction, find the novel strange and difficult. Its language is dense and the structure amorphous. Compared with the plot-driven Victorian novels that came before it, *To the Lighthouse* seems to have little in the way of action. Indeed, almost all of the events take place in the characters' minds.

Although *To the Lighthouse* is a radical departure from the nineteenth-century novel, it is, like its more traditional counterparts, intimately interested in developing characters and advancing both plot and themes. Woolf's experimentation has much to do with the time in which she lived: the turn of the century was marked by bold scientific developments. Charles Darwin's theory of evolution undermined an unquestioned faith in God that was, until that point, nearly universal, while the rise of psychoanalysis, a movement led by Sigmund Freud, introduced the idea of an unconscious mind. Such innovation in ways of scientific thinking had great influence on the styles and concerns of contemporary artists and writers like those in the Bloomsbury Group. *To the Lighthouse* exemplifies Woolf's style and many of her concerns as a novelist. With its characters based on her own parents and siblings, it is certainly her most autobiographical fictional statement, and in the characters of Mr. Ramsay, Mrs. Ramsay, and Lily Briscoe, Woolf offers some of her most penetrating explorations of the workings of the human consciousness as it perceives and analyzes, feels and interacts.

PLOT OVERVIEW

NOTE: To the Lighthouse *is divided into three sections: "The Window," "Time Passes," and "The Lighthouse." Each section is fragmented into stream-of-consciousness contributions from various narrators.*

"The Window" opens just before the start of World War I. Mr. Ramsay and Mrs. Ramsay bring their eight children to their summer home in the Hebrides (a group of islands west of Scotland). Across the bay from their house stands a large lighthouse. Six-year-old James Ramsay wants desperately to go to the lighthouse, and Mrs. Ramsay tells him that they will go the next day if the weather permits. James reacts gleefully, but Mr. Ramsay tells him coldly that the weather looks to be foul. James resents his father and believes that he enjoys being cruel to James and his siblings.

The Ramsays host a number of guests, including the dour Charles Tansley, who admires Mr. Ramsay's work as a metaphysical philosopher. Also at the house is Lily Briscoe, a young painter who begins a portrait of Mrs. Ramsay. Mrs. Ramsay wants Lily to marry William Bankes, an old friend of the Ramsays, but Lily resolves to remain single. Mrs. Ramsay does manage to arrange another marriage, however, between Paul Rayley and Minta Doyle, two of their acquaintances.

During the course of the afternoon, Paul proposes to Minta, Lily begins her painting, Mrs. Ramsay soothes the resentful James, and Mr. Ramsay frets over his shortcomings as a philosopher, periodically turning to Mrs. Ramsay for comfort. That evening, the Ramsays host a seemingly ill-fated dinner party. Paul and Minta are late returning from their walk on the beach with two of the Ramsays' children. Lily bristles at outspoken comments made by Charles Tansley, who suggests that women can neither paint nor write. Mr. Ramsay reacts rudely when Augustus Carmichael, a poet, asks for a second plate of soup. As the night draws on, however, these missteps right themselves, and the guests come together to make a memorable evening.

The joy, however, like the party itself, cannot last, and as Mrs. Ramsay leaves her guests in the dining room, she reflects that the event has already slipped into the past. Later, she joins her husband in the parlor. The couple sits quietly together, until Mr. Ramsay's characteristic insecurities interrupt their peace. He wants his wife to tell him that she loves him. Mrs. Ramsay is not one to make such pronouncements, but she concedes to his point made earlier in the day that the weather will be too rough for a trip to the lighthouse the next day. Mr. Ramsay thus knows that Mrs. Ramsay loves him. Night falls, and one night quickly becomes another.

Time passes more quickly as the novel enters the "Time Passes" segment. War breaks out across Europe. Mrs. Ramsay dies suddenly one night. Andrew Ramsay, her oldest son, is killed in battle, and his sister Prue dies from an illness related to childbirth. The family no longer vacations at its summerhouse, which falls into a state of disrepair: weeds take over the garden and spiders nest in the house. Ten years pass before the family returns. Mrs. McNab, the housekeeper, employs a few other women to help set the house in order. They rescue the house from oblivion and decay, and everything is in order when Lily Briscoe returns.

In "The Lighthouse" section, time returns to the slow detail of shifting points of view, similar in style to "The Window." Mr. Ramsay declares that he and James and Cam, one of his daughters, will journey to the lighthouse. On the morning of the voyage, delays throw him into a fit of temper. He appeals to Lily for sympathy, but, unlike Mrs. Ramsay, she is unable to provide him with what he needs. The Ramsays set off, and Lily takes her place on the lawn, determined to complete a painting she started but abandoned on her last visit. James and Cam bristle at their father's blustery behavior and are embarrassed by his constant self-pity. Still, as the boat reaches its destination, the children feel a fondness for him. Even James, whose skill as a sailor Mr. Ramsay praises, experiences a moment of connection with his father, though James so willfully resents him. Across the bay, Lily puts the finishing touch on her painting. She makes a definitive stroke on the canvas and puts her brush down, finally having achieved her vision.

CHARACTER LIST

Mrs. Ramsay Mr. Ramsay's wife. A beautiful and loving woman, Mrs. Ramsay is a wonderful hostess who takes pride in making memorable experiences for the guests at the family's summer home on the Isle of Skye. Affirming traditional gender roles wholeheartedly, she lavishes particular attention on her male guests, who she believes have delicate egos and need constant support and sympathy. She is a dutiful and loving wife but often struggles with her husband's difficult moods and selfishness. Without fail, however, she triumphs through these difficult times and demonstrates an ability to make something significant and lasting from the most ephemeral of circumstances, such as a dinner party.

Mr. Ramsay Mrs. Ramsay's husband, and a prominent metaphysical philosopher. Mr. Ramsay loves his family but often acts like something of a tyrant. He tends to be selfish and harsh due to his persistent personal and professional anxieties. He fears, more than anything, that his work is insignificant in the grand scheme of things and that he will not be remembered by future generations. Well aware of how blessed he is to have such a wonderful family, he nevertheless tends to punish his wife, children, and guests by demanding their constant sympathy, attention, and support.

Lily Briscoe A young, single painter who befriends the Ramsays on the Isle of Skye. Like Mr. Ramsay, Lily is plagued by fears that her work lacks worth. She begins a portrait of Mrs. Ramsay at the beginning of the novel but has trouble finishing it. The opinions of men like Charles Tansley, who insists that women cannot paint or write, threaten to undermine her confidence.

James Ramsay The Ramsays' youngest son. James loves his mother deeply and feels a murderous antipathy toward his father, with whom he must compete for Mrs. Ramsay's love and affection. At the beginning of the novel, Mr. Ramsay refuses the six-year-old James's request to go to the lighthouse, saying that the weather will be foul and not permit it; ten years later, James finally makes the journey with his father and his sister Cam. By this time, he has grown into a willful and moody young man who has much in common with his father, whom he detests.

Paul Rayley A young friend of the Ramsays who visits them on the Isle of Skye. Paul is a kind, impressionable young man who follows Mrs. Ramsay's wishes in marrying Minta Doyle.

Minta Doyle A flighty young woman who visits the Ramsays on the Isle of Skye. Minta marries Paul Rayley at Mrs. Ramsay's wishes.

Charles Tansley A young philosopher and pupil of Mr. Ramsay who stays with the Ramsays on the Isle of Skye. Tansley is a prickly and unpleasant man who harbors deep insecurities regarding his humble background. He often insults other people, particularly women such as Lily, whose talent and accomplishments he constantly calls into question. His bad behavior, like Mr. Ramsay's, is motivated by his need for reassurance.

William Bankes A botanist and old friend of the Ramsays who stays on the Isle of Skye. Bankes is a kind and mellow man whom Mrs. Ramsay hopes will marry Lily Briscoe. Although he never marries her, Bankes and Lily remain close friends.

Augustus Carmichael An opium-using poet who visits the Ramsays on the Isle of Skye. Carmichael languishes in literary obscurity until his verse becomes popular during the war.

Andrew Ramsay The oldest of the Ramsays' sons. Andrew is a competent, independent young man, and he looks forward to a career as a mathematician.

Jasper Ramsay One of the Ramsays' sons. Jasper, to his mother's chagrin, enjoys shooting birds.

Roger Ramsay One of the Ramsays' sons. Roger is wild and adventurous, like his sister Nancy.

Prue Ramsay The oldest Ramsay girl, a beautiful young woman. Mrs. Ramsay delights in contemplating Prue's marriage, which she believes will be blissful.

Rose Ramsay One of the Ramsays' daughters. Rose has a talent for making things beautiful. She arranges the fruit for her mother's dinner party and picks out her mother's jewelry.

Nancy Ramsay One of the Ramsays' daughters. Nancy accompanies Paul Rayley and Minta Doyle on their trip to the beach. Like her brother Roger, she is a wild adventurer.

Cam Ramsay One of the Ramsays' daughters. As a young girl, Cam is mischievous. She sails with James and Mr. Ramsay to the lighthouse in the novel's final section.

Mrs. McNab An elderly woman who takes care of the Ramsays' house on the Isle of Skye, restoring it after ten years of abandonment during and after World War I.

Macalister The fisherman who accompanies the Ramsays to the lighthouse. Macalister relates stories of shipwreck and maritime adventure to Mr. Ramsay and compliments James on his handling of the boat while James lands it at the lighthouse.

Macalister's boy The fisherman's boy. He rows James, Cam, and Mr. Ramsay to the lighthouse.

Analysis of Major Characters

Mrs. Ramsay

Mrs. Ramsay emerges from the novel's opening pages not only as a woman of great kindness and tolerance but also as a protector. Indeed, her primary goal is to preserve her youngest son James's sense of hope and wonder surrounding the lighthouse. Though she realizes (as James himself does) that Mr. Ramsay is correct in declaring that foul weather will ruin the next day's voyage, she persists in assuring James that the trip is a possibility. She does so not to raise expectations that will inevitably be dashed, but rather because she realizes that the beauties and pleasures of this world are ephemeral and should be preserved, protected, and cultivated as much as possible. So deep is this commitment that she behaves similarly to each of her guests, even those who do not deserve or appreciate her kindness. Before heading into town, for example, she insists on asking Augustus Carmichael, whom she senses does not like her, if she can bring him anything to make his stay more comfortable. Similarly, she tolerates the insufferable behavior of Charles Tansley, whose bitter attitude and awkward manners threaten to undo the delicate work she has done toward making a pleasant and inviting home.

As Lily Briscoe notes in the novel's final section, Mrs. Ramsay feels the need to play this role primarily in the company of men. Indeed, Mrs. Ramsay feels obliged to protect the entire opposite sex. According to her, men shoulder the burden of ruling countries and managing economies. Their important work, she believes, leaves them vulnerable and in need of constant reassurance, a service that women can and should provide. Although this dynamic fits squarely into traditional gender boundaries, it is important to note the strength that Mrs. Ramsay feels. At several points, she is aware of her own power, and her posture is far from that of a submissive woman. At the same time, interjections of domesticated anxiety, such as her refrain of "the bill for the greenhouse would be fifty pounds," undercut this power.

Ultimately, as is evident from her meeting with Mr. Ramsay at the close of "The Window," Mrs. Ramsay never compromises herself. Here, she is able—masterfully—to satisfy her husband's desire for her to tell him she loves him without saying the words she finds so difficult to say. This scene displays Mrs. Ramsay's ability to bring together disparate things into a whole. In a world marked by the ravages of time and war, in which everything must and will fall apart, there is perhaps no greater gift than a sense of unity, even if it is only temporary. Lily and other characters find themselves grasping for this unity after Mrs. Ramsay's death.

MR. RAMSAY

Mr. Ramsay stands, in many respects, as Mrs. Ramsay's opposite. Whereas she acts patiently, kindly, and diplomatically toward others, he tends to be short-tempered, selfish, and rude. Woolf fittingly describes him as "lean as a knife, narrow as the blade of one," which conjures both his physical presence and suggests the sharpness (and violence) of his personality. An accomplished metaphysician who made an invaluable contribution to his field as a young man, Mr. Ramsay bears out his wife's philosophy regarding gender: men, burdened by the importance of their own work, need to seek out the comforts and assurances of women. Throughout the novel, Mr. Ramsay implores his wife and even his guests for sympathy. Mr. Ramsay is uncertain about the fate of his work and its legacy, and his insecurity manifests itself either as a weapon or a weakness. His keen awareness of death's inevitability motivates him to dash the hopes of young James and to bully Mrs. Ramsay into declaring her love for him. This hyperawareness also forces him to confront his own mortality and face the possibility that he, like the forgotten books and plates that litter the second part of the novel, might sink into oblivion.

LILY BRISCOE

Lily is a passionate artist, and, like Mr. Ramsay, she worries over the fate of her work, fearing that her paintings will be hung in attics or tossed absentmindedly under a couch. Conventional femininity, represented by Mrs. Ramsay in the form of marriage and family, confounds Lily, and she rejects it. The recurring memory of Charles Tansley insisting that women can neither paint nor write deepens her anxiety. It is with these self-doubts that she begins her portrait of Mrs. Ramsay at the beginning of the novel, a portrait riddled with problems that she is unable to solve. But Lily undergoes a drastic transformation over the course of the novel, evolving from a woman who cannot make sense of the shapes and colors that she tries to reproduce into an artist who achieves her vision and, more important, overcomes the anxieties that have kept her from it. By the end of the novel, Lily, a serious and diligent worker, puts into practice all that she has learned from Mrs. Ramsay. Much like the woman she so greatly admires, she is able to craft something beautiful and lasting from the ephemeral materials around her—the changing light, the view of the bay. Her artistic achievement suggests a larger sense of completeness in that she finally feels united with Mr. Ramsay and the rational, intellectual sphere that he represents.

JAMES RAMSAY

A sensitive child, James is gripped by a love for his mother that is as overpowering and complete as his hatred for his father. He feels a murderous rage against Mr. Ramsay, who, he believes, delights in delivering the news that there will be no trip to the lighthouse. But James grows into a young man who shares many of his father's characteristics, the same ones that incited such anger in him as a child. When he eventually sails to the lighthouse with his father, James, like Mr. Ramsay, is withdrawn, moody, and easily offended. His need to be praised, as noted by his sister Cam, mirrors his father's incessant need for sympathy, reassurance, and love. Indeed, as they approach the lighthouse, James considers his father's profile and recognizes the profound loneliness that stamps both of their personalities. By the time the boat lands, James's attitude toward his father has changed considerably. As he softens toward Mr. Ramsay and comes to accept him as he is, James, like Lily, who finishes her painting on shore at that very moment, achieves a rare, fleeting moment in which the world seems blissfully whole and complete.

Themes, Motifs & Symbols

Themes

Themes are the fundamental and often universal ideas explored in a literary work.

The Transience of Life and Work

Mr. Ramsay and Mrs. Ramsay take completely different approaches to life: he relies on his intellect, while she depends on her emotions. But they share the knowledge that the world around them is transient—that nothing lasts forever. Mr. Ramsay reflects that even the most enduring of reputations, such as Shakespeare's, are doomed to eventual oblivion. This realization accounts for the bitter aspect of his character. Frustrated by the inevitable demise of his own body of work and envious of the few geniuses who will outlast him, he plots to found a school of philosophy that argues that the world is designed for the average, unadorned man, for the "liftman in the Tube" rather than for the rare immortal writer.

Mrs. Ramsay is as keenly aware as her husband of the passage of time and of mortality. She recoils, for instance, at the notion of James growing into an adult, registers the world's many dangers, and knows that no one, not even her husband, can protect her from them. Her reaction to this knowledge is markedly different from her husband's. Whereas Mr. Ramsay is bowed by the weight of his own demise, Mrs. Ramsay is fueled with the need to make precious and memorable whatever time she has on earth. Such crafted moments, she reflects, offer the only hope of something that endures.

Art as a Means of Preservation

In the face of an existence that is inherently without order or meaning, Mr. and Mrs. Ramsay employ different strategies for making their lives significant. Mr. Ramsay devotes himself to his progression through the course of human thought, while Mrs. Ramsay cultivates memorable experiences from social interactions. Neither of these strategies, however, proves an adequate means of preserving one's experience. After all, Mr. Ramsay fails to obtain the philosophical understanding he so desperately desires, and Mrs. Ramsay's life, though filled with moments that have the shine and resilience of rubies, ends. Only Lily Briscoe finds a way to preserve her experience, and that way is through her art. As Lily begins her portrait of Mrs. Ramsay at the beginning of the novel, Woolf notes the scope of the project: Lily means to order and connect elements that have no necessary relation in the world—"hedges and houses and mothers and children." By the end of the novel, ten years later, Lily finishes the painting she started, which stands as a moment of clarity wrested from confusion. Art is, perhaps, the only hope of surety in a world destined and determined to change: for, while mourning Mrs. Ramsay's death and painting on the lawn, Lily reflects that "nothing stays, all changes; but not words, not paint."

The Subjective Nature of Reality

Toward the end of the novel, Lily reflects that in order to see Mrs. Ramsay clearly—to understand her character completely—she would need at least fifty pairs of eyes; only then would she be privy to every possible angle and nuance. The truth, according to this assertion, rests in the accumulation of different, even opposing vantage points. Woolf's technique in structuring the story mirrors Lily's assertion. She is committed to creating a sense of the world that not only depends upon the private perceptions of her characters but is also *nothing more than* the accumulation of those perceptions. To try to reimagine the story as told from a single character's perspective or—in the tradition of the Victorian novelists—from the author's perspective is to realize the radical scope and difficulty of Woolf's project.

The Restorative Effects of Beauty

At the beginning of the novel, both Mr. Ramsay and Lily Briscoe are drawn out of moments of irritation by an image of extreme beauty. The image, in both cases, is a vision of Mrs. Ramsay, who, as she sits reading with James, is a sight powerful enough to incite "rapture" in William Bankes. Beauty retains this soothing effect throughout the novel: something as trifling as a large but very beautiful arrangement of fruit can, for a moment, assuage the discomfort of the guests at Mrs. Ramsay's dinner party.

Lily later complicates the notion of beauty as restorative by suggesting that beauty has the unfortunate consequence of simplifying the truth. Her impression of Mrs. Ramsay, she believes, is compromised by a determination to view her as beautiful and to smooth over her complexities and faults. Nevertheless, Lily continues on her quest to "still" or "freeze" a moment from life and make it beautiful. Although the vision of an isolated moment is necessarily incomplete, it is lasting and, as such, endlessly seductive to her.

Motifs

Motifs are recurring structures, contrasts, or literary devices that can help to develop and inform the text's major themes.

The Differing Behaviors of Men and Women
As Lily Briscoe suffers through Charles Tansley's boorish opinions about women and art, she reflects that human relations are worst between men and women. Indeed, given the extremely opposite ways in which men and women behave throughout the novel, this difficulty is no wonder. The dynamic between the sexes is best understood by considering the behavior of Mr. and Mrs. Ramsay. Their constant conflict has less to do with divergent philosophies—indeed, they both acknowledge and are motivated by the same fear of mortality—than with the way they process that fear. Men, Mrs. Ramsay reflects in the opening pages of the novel, bow to it. Given her rather traditional notions of gender roles, she excuses her husband's behavior as inevitable, asking how men can be expected to settle the political and economic business of nations and not suffer doubts. This understanding attitude places on women the responsibility for soothing men's damaged egos and achieving some kind of harmony (even if temporary) with them. Lily Briscoe, who as a single woman represents a social order more radial and lenient than Mrs. Ramsay's, resists this duty but ultimately caves in to it.

Brackets
In "Time Passes," brackets surround the few sentences recounting the deaths of Prue and Andrew Ramsay, while in "The Lighthouse," brackets surround the sentences comprising Chapter VI. Each set of sentences in brackets in the earlier section contains violence, death, and the destruction of potential; the short, stabbing accounts accentuate the brutality of these events. But in Chapter VI of "The Lighthouse," the purpose of the brackets changes from indicating violence and death to violence and potential survival. Whereas in

"Time Passes," the brackets surround Prue's death in childbirth and Andrew's perishing in war, in "The Lighthouse" they surround the "mutilated" but "alive still" body of a fish.

SYMBOLS

Symbols are objects, characters, figures, or colors used to represent abstract ideas or concepts.

THE LIGHTHOUSE

Lying across the bay and meaning something different and intimately personal to each character, the lighthouse is at once inaccessible, illuminating, and infinitely interpretable. As the destination from which the novel takes its title, the lighthouse suggests that the destinations that seem surest are most unobtainable. Just as Mr. Ramsay is certain of his wife's love for him and aims to hear her speak words to that end in "The Window," Mrs. Ramsay finds these words impossible to say. These failed attempts to arrive at some sort of solid ground, like Lily's first try at painting Mrs. Ramsay or Mrs. Ramsay's attempt to see Paul and Minta married, result only in more attempts, further excursions rather than rest. The lighthouse stands as a potent symbol of this lack of attainability. James arrives only to realize that it is not at all the mist-shrouded destination of his childhood. Instead, he is made to reconcile two competing and contradictory images of the tower—how it appeared to him when he was a boy and how it appears to him now that he is a man. He decides that both of these images contribute to the essence of the lighthouse—that nothing is ever only one thing—a sentiment that echoes the novel's determination to arrive at truth through varied and contradictory vantage points.

LILY'S PAINTING

Lily's painting represents a struggle against gender convention, represented by Charles Tansley's statement that women can't paint or write. Lily's desire to express Mrs. Ramsay's essence as a wife and mother in the painting mimics the impulse among modern women to know and understand intimately the gendered experiences of the women who came before them. Lily's composition attempts to discover and comprehend Mrs. Ramsay's beauty just as Woolf's construction of Mrs. Ramsay's character reflects her attempts to access and portray her own mother.

The painting also represents dedication to a feminine artistic vision, expressed through Lily's anxiety over showing it to William Bankes. In deciding that completing the painting regardless of what happens to it is the most important thing, Lily makes the choice to establish her own artistic voice. In the end, she decides that her vision depends on balance and synthesis: how to bring together disparate things in harmony. In this respect, her project mirrors Woolf's writing, which synthesizes the perceptions of her many characters to come to a balanced and truthful portrait of the world.

The Ramsays' House

The Ramsays' house is a stage where Woolf and her characters explain their beliefs and observations. During her dinner party, Mrs. Ramsay sees her house display her own inner notions of shabbiness and her inability to preserve beauty. In the "Time Passes" section, the ravages of war and destruction and the passage of time are reflected in the condition of the house rather than in the emotional development or observable aging of the characters. The house stands in for the collective consciousness of those who stay in it. At times the characters long to escape it, while at other times it serves as refuge. From the dinner party to the journey to the lighthouse, Woolf shows the house from every angle, and its structure and contents mirror the interior of the characters who inhabit it.

The Sea

References to the sea appear throughout the novel. Broadly, the ever-changing, ever-moving waves parallel the constant forward movement of time and the changes it brings. Woolf describes the sea lovingly and beautifully, but her most evocative depictions of it point to its violence. As a force that brings destruction, has the power to decimate islands, and, as Mr. Ramsay reflects, "eats away the ground we stand on," the sea is a powerful reminder of the impermanence and delicacy of human life and accomplishments.

The Boar's Skull

After her dinner party, Mrs. Ramsay retires upstairs to find the children wide-awake, bothered by the boar's skull that hangs on the nursery wall. The presence of the skull acts as a disturbing reminder that death is always at hand, even (or perhaps especially) during life's most blissful moments.

SYMBOLS

THE FRUIT BASKET

Rose arranges a fruit basket for her mother's dinner party that serves to draw the partygoers out of their private suffering and unite them. Although Augustus Carmichael and Mrs. Ramsay appreciate the arrangement differently—he rips a bloom from it; she refuses to disturb it—the pair is brought harmoniously, if briefly, together. The basket testifies both to the "frozen" quality of beauty that Lily describes and to beauty's seductive and soothing quality.

Summary & Analysis

The Window: Chapters I–IV

Summary: Chapter I

Mr. and Mrs. Ramsay are staying at their summerhouse in the Hebrides with their eight children and several houseguests. James, the Ramsays' youngest child, sits on the floor carefully cutting out pictures from the Army and Navy Stores catalogue. Mrs. Ramsay assures James he will be able to visit the nearby lighthouse the following day if weather permits, but Mr. Ramsay interjects that the weather will not allow it. Six-year-old James feels a murderous rage against his father for ridiculing his mother, whom James considers "ten thousand times better in every way." Mrs. Ramsay tries to assure James that the weather may well be fine, but Charles Tansley, a stiff intellectual who greatly respects Mr. Ramsay, disagrees.

Tansley's insensitivity toward James irritates Mrs. Ramsay, but she tries to act warmly toward her male houseguests, forbidding her irreverent daughters to mock Tansley. After lunch, Mrs. Ramsay invites Tansley to accompany her on an errand into town, and he accepts. On their way out, she stops to ask Augustus Carmichael, an elderly poet also staying with the Ramsays, if he needs anything, but he responds that he does not. On the way into town, Mrs. Ramsay tells Carmichael's story. He was once a promising poet and intellectual, but he made an unfortunate marriage. Mrs. Ramsay's confidence flatters Tansley, and he rambles incessantly about his work.

The two pass a sign advertising a circus, and Mrs. Ramsay suggests that they all go. Hesitant, Tansley explains to Mrs. Ramsay that, having grown up in an impoverished family, he was never taken to a circus. Mrs. Ramsay reflects that Tansley harbors a deep insecurity regarding his humble background and that this insecurity causes much of his unpleasantness. She now feels more kindly toward him, though his self-centered talk continues to bore her. Tansley, however, thinks that Mrs. Ramsay is the most beautiful woman he has ever seen. Like most of her male guests, he is a little in love with her. Even the chance to carry her bag thrills him.

SUMMARY: CHAPTER II

Later that evening, Tansley looks out the window and announces gently, for Mrs. Ramsay's sake, that there will be no trip to the lighthouse tomorrow. Mrs. Ramsay finds him tedious and annoying.

SUMMARY: CHAPTER III

Mrs. Ramsay comforts James, telling him that the sun may well shine in the morning. She listens to the men talking outside, but when their conversation stops, she receives a sudden shock from the sound of the waves rolling against the shore. Normally the waves seem to steady and support her, but occasionally they make her think of destruction, death, and the passage of time. The sound of her husband reciting to himself Alfred, Lord Tennyson's poem "The Charge of the Light Brigade" returns to her the sense that all is right with the world. She notices Lily Briscoe painting on the edge of the lawn and remembers that she is supposed to keep her head still for Lily, who is painting her portrait.

SUMMARY: CHAPTER IV

As Mr. Ramsay passes Lily on the grass, he nearly tips over her easel. Lily's old friend William Bankes, who rents a room near hers in the village, joins her on the grass. Sensing that they have somehow intruded on their host's privacy, Lily and Bankes are both slightly unnerved by the sight of Mr. Ramsay thundering about talking to himself. Lily struggles to capture her vision on canvas, a project, she reflects, that keeps her from declaring outright her love for Mrs. Ramsay, the house, and the entire scene.

Bankes, who once enjoyed an intimate relationship with Mr. Ramsay, now feels somewhat removed from him. He cannot understand why Mr. Ramsay needs so much attention and praise. Bankes criticizes this facet of Ramsay's personality, but Lily reminds him of the importance of Mr. Ramsay's work. Lily has never quite grasped the content of Mr. Ramsay's philosophy, although Andrew, the Ramsays' oldest son, once helpfully likened his father's work on "the nature of reality" to thinking about a kitchen table when one is not there. Lily finds Mr. Ramsay at once otherworldly and ridiculous. When Mr. Ramsay realizes that Lily and Bankes have been watching him, he is embarrassed to have been caught acting out the poem so theatrically, but he stifles his embarrassment and pretends to be unruffled.

Analysis — The Window: Chapters I–IV

Virginia Woolf read the work of Sigmund Freud, whose revolutionary model of human psychology explored the unconscious mind and raised questions regarding internal versus external realities. Woolf opens *To the Lighthouse* by dramatizing one of Freud's more popular theories, the Oedipal conflict. Freud turned to the ancient Greek story of Oedipus, who inadvertently kills his father and marries his mother, to structure his thoughts on both family dynamics and male sexual development. According to Freud, young boys tend to demand and monopolize their mothers' love at the risk of incurring the jealousy and wrath of their fathers. Between young James Ramsay and his parents, we see a similar triangle formed: James adores his mother as completely as he resents his father. Woolf's gesture to Freud testifies to the radical nature of her project. As much a visionary as Freud, Woolf set out to write a novel that mapped the psychological unconscious. Instead of chronicling the many things characters say and do to one another, she concentrated on the innumerable things that exist beneath the surface of speech and action.

Achieving this goal required the development of an innovative method of writing that came to be known as stream of consciousness, which charts the interior thoughts, perceptions, and feelings of one or more characters. Although interior monologue is another term often used to refer to this technique, an important difference exists between the two. While both stream of consciousness and interior monologue describe a character's interior life, the latter does so by using the character's grammar and syntax. In other words, the character's thoughts are transcribed directly, without an authorial voice acting as mediator. Woolf does not make use of interior monologue; throughout *To the Lighthouse,* she maintains a voice distinct and distant from those of her characters. The pattern of young James's mind, for instance, is described in the same lush language as that of his mother and father. It is more apt to say, then, that the novel is *about* the stream of human consciousness—the complex connection between feelings and memories—rather than a literary representation of it.

Through these forays into each character's mind, Woolf explores the different ways in which individuals search for and create meaning in their own experience. She strives to express how individuals order their perceptions into a coherent understanding of life. This endeavor becomes particularly important in a world in which life no longer has any inherent meaning. Darwin's theory of evolution, published in 1859 in *The Origin of Species,* challenged the then universal belief that human life was divinely inspired and, as such, intrinsically significant. Each of the three main characters has a different approach to establishing the worth of his or her life. Mr. Ramsay represents an intellectual approach; as a metaphysical philosopher, he relies on his work to secure his reputation. Mrs. Ramsay, devoted to family, friends, and the sanctity of social order, relies on her emotions rather than her mind to lend lasting meaning to her experiences. Lily, hoping to capture and preserve the truth of a single instant on canvas, uses her art.

THE WINDOW: CHAPTERS V–VIII

> [W]ho will blame him if he does homage to the beauty
> of the world?   (See QUOTATIONS, p. 51)

SUMMARY: CHAPTER V

At the house, Mrs. Ramsay inspects the stocking she has been knitting for the lighthouse keeper's son, just in case the weather allows them to go to the lighthouse the next day. Mrs. Ramsay thinks about her children and her tasks as a mother. She also recollects her father's death. Mr. Bankes reflects upon Mrs. Ramsay's beauty, which he cannot completely understand. She is, he thinks, much like the walls of the unfinished hotel he watches being built in back of his home. Mr. Bankes sees more than aesthetic beauty in her, "the quivering thing, the living thing." Mrs. Ramsay goes on knitting the stocking for the little boy, and lovingly urges James to cut another picture from the Army and Navy Stores catalogue.

SUMMARY: CHAPTER VI

Mr. Ramsay approaches his wife. He is petulant and needs reassurance after his embarrassment in front of Lily and Bankes. When Mrs. Ramsay tells him that she is preparing a stocking for the lighthouse keeper's boy, Mr. Ramsay becomes infuriated by what he sees as her extraordinary irrationality. His sense of safety restored, Mr. Ramsay resumes his strolling on the lawn, giving himself over to the "energies of his splendid mind." He thinks to himself that the progress of human thought is analogous to the alphabet—each successive concept represents a letter, and every individual struggles in his life to make it through as many letters as he can. Mr. Ramsay thinks that he has plodded from A to Q with great effort but feels that R now eludes him. He reflects that not many men can reach even Q, and that only one man in the course of a generation can reach Z. There are two types of great thinkers, he notes: those who work their way from A to Z diligently, and those few geniuses who simply arrive at Z in a single instant. Mr. Ramsay knows he does not belong to the latter type, and resolves (or hopes) to fight his way to Z. Still, he fears that his reputation will fade after his death. He reminds himself that all fame is fleeting and that a single stone will outlast Shakespeare. But he hates to think that he has made little real, lasting difference in the world.

SUMMARY: CHAPTER VII

James, reading with his mother, senses his father's presence and hates him. Discerning his father's need for sympathy, he wishes his father would leave him alone with his mother. Mr. Ramsay declares himself a failure, and Mrs. Ramsay, recognizing his need to be assured of his genius, tells him that Tansley considers him the greatest living philosopher. Eventually, she restores his confidence, and he goes off to watch the children play cricket. Mrs. Ramsay returns to the story that she is reading to James. Inwardly, she reflects anxiously that people observing her interactions with Mr. Ramsay might infer that her husband depends on her excessively and think mistakenly that her contributions to the world surpass his. Augustus Carmichael shuffles past.

SUMMARY: CHAPTER VIII

Carmichael, an opium addict, ignores Mrs. Ramsay, hurting her feelings and her pride. She realizes, however, that her kindness is petty because she expects to receive gratitude and admiration from those she treats with sympathy and generosity. Still troubled, Mr. Ramsay wanders across the lawn, mulling over the progress and fate of civilization and great men, wondering if the world would be different if Shakespeare had never existed. He believes that a "slave class" of unadorned, unacknowledged workers must exist for the good of society. The thought displeases him, and he resolves to argue that the world exists for such human beings, for the men who operate the London subway rather than for immortal writers.

He reaches the edge of the lawn and looks out at the bay. As the waves wash against the shore, Mr. Ramsay finds the encroaching waters to be an apt metaphor for human ignorance, which always seems to eat away what little is known with certainty. He turns from this depressing thought to stare at the image of his wife and child, which makes him realize that he is primarily happy, even though "he had not done that thing he might have done."

ANALYSIS — THE WINDOW: CHAPTERS V–VIII

The line of poetry that Mr. Ramsay recites as he blusters across the lawn is taken from Tennyson's "Charge of the Light Brigade." The poem, which tells of 600 soldiers marching bravely to their death, ends with the lines

> When can their glory fade?
> O the wild charge they made!
> All the world wonder'd.
> Honour the charge they made!

A meditation on immortality, the poem captures the tumultuous state of Mr. Ramsay's mind and his anxiety about whether he and his work will be remembered by future generations. Here, Mr. Ramsay emerges as an uncompromising but terribly insecure intellectual. He knows the world almost exclusively through words, so he tries to express and mediate his sadness with the lines by Tennyson. He yearns for the "glory" and the "wild charge" of which the poem speaks in the form of brilliant contributions to philosophy. Although he acknowledges a more profound truth—that in the end no immortality exists, and even a stone will outlast a figure as influential as William Shakespeare—Mr. Ramsay cannot help but indulge his need to be comforted, to have others assure him of his place in the world and its importance. The posture he assumes as he approaches his wife in Chapter VII is one that he returns to often. Again and again, he displays a relentless desire for sympathy and understanding from her.

Mr. Ramsay is not alone in his need for his wife's affections. Through Mrs. Ramsay, Woolf suggests that Mr. Ramsay's traits belong to all men. Charles Tansley exhibits similar behavior in the opening chapters. He navigates the world according to what he has studied and read, and lashes out with "the fatal sterility of the male" for fear that his contributions will be deemed lacking. Mrs. Ramsay believes such daunted and insecure behavior to be inevitable, given the importance of men's concerns and work. She sees men as well as women forced into roles that prescribe their behavior. In her extended sympathy for her husband and in her attempts at match-making, Mrs. Ramsay recognizes and observes these roles while try-ing to make it less painful for the people in her life to have to play them. This question of gender roles, which occupies much space in the coming chapters, is played out most fully in the relationship between Mrs. Ramsay and Lily Briscoe. Mrs. Ramsay's maternal and wifely devotion represents the kind of traditional lifestyle to which Lily Briscoe refuses to conform.

Mr. Ramsay, who is obsessed with understanding and advancing the process of human thought, reveals the novel's concern with knowledge. *To the Lighthouse* asks how humanity acquires knowl-edge and questions the scope and validity of that knowledge. The fact that Mr. Ramsay, who is decidedly one of the eminent philoso-phers of his day, doubts the solidity of his own thoughts suggests that a purely rational, universally agreed-upon worldview is an impossibility. Indeed, one of the effects of Woolf's narrative method is to suggest that objective reality does not exist. The ever-shifting viewpoints that she employs construct a world in which reality is merely a collection of subjectively determined truths.

THE WINDOW: CHAPTERS IX–XI

[F]or it was not knowledge but unity that she desired, not inscriptions on tablets, nothing that could be written in any language known to men, but intimacy itself. . . . (See QUOTATIONS, p. 52)

SUMMARY: CHAPTER IX

William Bankes considers Mr. Ramsay's behavior and concludes that it is a pity that his old friend cannot act more conventionally. He suggests to Lily, who stands beside him putting away her paint and brushes, that their host is something of a hypocrite. Lily disagrees with him. Though she finds Mr. Ramsay narrow and self-absorbed, she also observes the sincerity with which he seeks admi-ration. Lily is about to speak and criticize Mrs. Ramsay, but Bankes's "rapture" of watching Mrs. Ramsay silences her. As he stares at Mrs. Ramsay, it is obvious to Lily that he is in love. The rapture of his gaze touches her, so much so that she lets Bankes look at her painting, which she considers to be dreadfully bad. She thinks of Charles Tansley's claim that women cannot paint or write.

Lily remembers the criticism she was about to make of Mrs. Ramsay, whom she resents for insinuating that she, Lily, as an unmarried woman, cannot know the best of life. Lily reflects on the essence of Mrs. Ramsay, which she is trying to paint, and insists that she herself was not made for marriage. She muses, with some distress, that no one can ever know anything about anyone, because people are separate and cut off from one another. She hopes to counter this phenomenon and achieve unity with, and knowledge of, others through her art. By painting, she hopes to attain a kind of intimacy that will bring her closer to the world outside her consciousness.

Lily braces herself as Bankes looks over her portrait of Mrs. Ramsay and James. She discusses the painting with him. As they talk about the shadows, light, and the purple triangle meant to represent Mrs. Ramsay, Lily wonders how to connect them and make them whole. She also feels that Bankes has taken her painting from her by looking at it and that they have shared something intimate.

SUMMARY: CHAPTER X

Cam Ramsay, Mrs. and Mr. Ramsay's devilish daughter, rushes past and nearly knocks the easel over. Mrs. Ramsay calls to Cam, asking after Paul Rayley, Minta Doyle, and Andrew, who have not returned from their walk on the beach. Mrs. Ramsay assumes that this delay means that Paul has proposed to Minta, which is what she intended when she orchestrated the walk. A clever matchmaker, Mrs. Ramsay has been accused of being domineering, but she feels justified in her efforts because she truly likes Minta. She feels that Minta must accept the time that she and Paul have spent alone together recently.

Mrs. Ramsay believes that she would be domineering in pursuit of social causes. She feels passionately that the island needs a hospital and a dairy, but rationalizes that she can further these goals once her children grow older. Still, she resists the passage of time, wishing that her children would stay young forever and her family as happy as it now is. Mrs. Ramsay further meditates about life, realizing a kind of transactional relationship between it and herself. She lists social problems and intersperses them with personal anxieties, noting, for instance, that "the bill for the greenhouse would be fifty pounds." This anxiety extends to her thoughts of Paul and Minta, thinking that perhaps marriage and family are an escape that not everyone needs. She finishes reading James his story, and the nursemaid takes him to bed. Mrs. Ramsay is certain that he is thinking of their thwarted trip to the lighthouse and that he will remember not being able to go for the rest of his life.

SUMMARY: CHAPTER XI

Alone, Mrs. Ramsay knits and gazes out at the lighthouse, thinking that children never forget harsh words or disappointments. She enjoys her respite from being and doing, since she finds peace only when she is no longer herself. Without personality, in a "wedge-shaped core of darkness," she rids herself of worry. She suddenly becomes sad, and thinks that no God could have made a world in which happiness is so fleeting and in which reason, order, and justice are so overwhelmed by suffering and death. From a distance, Mr. Ramsay sees her and notices her sadness and beauty. He wants to protect her, but hesitates, feeling helpless and reflecting that his temper causes her grief. He resolves not to interrupt her, but soon enough, sensing his desire to protect her, Mrs. Ramsay calls after him, takes up her shawl, and meets him on the lawn.

ANALYSIS — THE WINDOW: CHAPTERS IX–XI

While Mrs. Ramsay's reliance on intuition contrasts with her husband's aloofness and self-interest, she shares with him a dread of mortality. Mrs. Ramsay's mind seizes "the fact that there is no reason, order, justice." It is only in her "wedge-shaped core of darkness" that she escapes "being and doing" enough to be herself. She realizes that happiness is, without exception, fleeting and ephemeral. Refrains of "children never forget" and "the greenhouse would cost fifty pounds" and other expressions of domestic anxiety break into her peace and solitude and advance the notion that life is transactional. However, it is exactly this awareness of death and worry that make her moments of wholeness so precious to her. Her sense of the inevitability of suffering and death lead her to search for such moments of bliss.

According to Mr. Ramsay's conception of human thought, Mrs. Ramsay may not be as far along in the alphabet as he, but she has surpassed her husband in one important respect. Unlike Mr. Ramsay, she is able to move beyond the "treacheries" of the world by accepting them. Mr. Ramsay, on the other hand, becomes so mired in the thought of his own mortality that he is rendered helpless and dependent upon his wife.

Lily's complicated reaction to Mrs. Ramsay in this section advances the novel's discussion of gender by introducing a character who lives outside accepted gender conventions. As a single woman who, much to Mrs. Ramsay's chagrin, shows little interest in marrying, Lily represents a new and evolving social order and raises the suspicions of several characters. Mrs. Ramsay suggests that she cannot know life completely until she has married, while Charles Tansley insists that women were not made to be painters or writers. Lily's refusal to bow to these notions, however, testifies to her commitment to living as an independent woman and an artist. Indeed, by rejecting these once universally held beliefs, Lily creates a parallel between her life and her art. On canvas, she does not mean to make an assertion of objective truth; instead, she hopes to capture and preserve a moment that appears real to her. Her determination to live her life according to her own principles demands as great a struggle and commitment as her painting.

Woolf's pairing of Lily with Mrs. Ramsay highlights her interest in the relationships among women outside the realm of prescribed gender roles. Mrs. Ramsay takes on the conventional roles of wife and mother and accepts the suffering and anxiety they bring. At the same time, she remains aware of her power: "Was she not forgetting how strongly she influenced people?" Lily rejects gender conventions, but she remains plagued by artistic self-doubt and feels that others' notice of her work somehow takes the work away from her. Woolf uses the relationship between these women to show the detrimental effect of male society on female artistic vision, and to illustrate the potential intimacy and complexity of such relationships.

THE WINDOW: CHAPTERS XII–XVI

SUMMARY: CHAPTER XII

As they walk together, Mrs. Ramsay brings up to Mr. Ramsay her worries about their son Jasper's proclivity for shooting birds and her disagreement with Mr. Ramsay's high opinion of Charles Tansley. She complains about Tansley's bullying and excessive discussion of his dissertation; Mr. Ramsay counters that his dissertation is all that Tansley has in his life. He adds that he would disinherit their daughter Prue if she married Tansley, however. They continue walking, and the conversation turns to their children. They discuss Prue's beauty and Andrew's promise as a student. Still walking, they reach a conversational impasse reflecting a deeper emotional distance. Mr. Ramsay mourns that the best and most productive period of his career is over, but he chastises himself for his sadness, thinking that his wife and eight children are, in their own way, a fine contribution to "the poor little universe." Her husband and his moods amaze Mrs. Ramsay, who realizes that he believes that his books would have been better had he not had children. Impressive as his thoughts are, she wonders if he notices the ordinary things in life such as the view or the flowers. She notices a star on the horizon and wants to point it out to her husband, but stops. The sight, she knows, will somehow only sadden him. Lily comes into view with William Bankes, and Mrs. Ramsay decides that the couple must marry.

Summary: Chapter XIII

Lily listens to William Bankes describe the art he has seen while visiting Europe. She reflects on the number of great paintings she has never seen but decides that not having seen them is probably best since other artists' work tends to make one disappointed with one's own. The couple turns to see Mr. and Mrs. Ramsay watching Prue and Jasper playing ball. The Ramsays become, for Lily, a symbol of married life. As the couples meet on the lawn, Lily can tell that Mrs. Ramsay intends for her to marry Bankes. Lily suddenly feels a sense of space and of things having been blown apart. Mrs. Ramsay worries since Paul Rayley and Minta Doyle have not yet returned from their walk and asks if the Ramsays' daughter Nancy accompanied them.

Summary: Chapter XIV

Nancy, at Minta's request and out of a sense of obligation, has accompanied Minta and Paul on their walk. Nancy wonders what Minta wants as she keeps taking then dropping Nancy's hand. Andrew appreciates the way Minta walks, wearing more sensible clothes than most women and taking risks that most women will not. Still, this outing disappoints Andrew. In the end, he does not like taking women on walks or the chummy way that Paul claps him on the back. The group reaches the beach and Nancy explores the tiny pools left by the ebb tide. Andrew and Nancy come upon Paul and Minta kissing, which irritates them. Upon leaving the beach, Minta discovers that she has lost her grandmother's brooch. Everyone searches for it as the tide rolls in. Wanting to prove his worth,

Paul resolves to leave the house early tomorrow morning in order to scour the beach for the brooch. He thinks with disappointment on the moment he asked Minta to marry him. He considers admitting this disappointment to Mrs. Ramsay, who, he believes, forced him into proposing, but, as the well-lit house comes into view, he decides not to make a fool of himself.

SUMMARY: CHAPTER XV
Prue, in answer to her mother's question, replies that she thinks that Nancy did accompany Paul and Minta.

SUMMARY: CHAPTER XVI
As Mrs. Ramsay dresses for dinner, she wonders if Nancy's presence will distract Paul from proposing to Minta. Mrs. Ramsay lets her daughter Rose choose her jewelry for the evening, a ceremony that somehow saddens her. She becomes increasingly distressed by Paul and Minta's tardiness, worrying for their safety and fearing that dinner will be ruined. Eventually she hears the group return from its walk and feels annoyed. Everyone assembles in the dinning room for dinner.

ANALYSIS—THE WINDOW: CHAPTERS XII–XVI
Woolf's disjointed story line would have been especially shocking to readers raised on Victorian novels, who were used to linear narratives, elaborate plots, and the mediating voice of an author. Woolf eliminates these traditional narrative elements and presents her characters' competing visions of reality. As Mr. and Mrs. Ramsay stroll on the lawn, for instance, Woolf forces us to weigh and judge their various perceptions. Mr. and Mrs. Ramsay's viewpoints conflict over whether it is more important to publish a remarkable dissertation or to have the ability to "notice his own daughter's beauty, or whether there was pudding on his plate of roast beef." She portrays Mr. Ramsay's cold, domineering neuroses as completely as Mrs. Ramsay's generosity and love. Woolf's goal is not to present one character's experience as the truth but rather to bring opposing worldviews and visions of reality, such as those held by the Ramsays, into a unified story.

Woolf does not describe Mr. Ramsay's philosophical work or the work he admires. Earlier, Lily recalls Andrew's likening of his father's work to musings over a kitchen table, and here Mrs. Ram-

SUMMARY & ANALYSIS

say summarizes the philosophy of Charles Tansley as dealing with "the influence of somebody upon something." While the brevity of these descriptions seems dismissive, Woolf takes her characters' work and anxieties seriously. Woolf rejects not Mr. Ramsay but rather preconceived notions about what a novel should be. Woolf, along with James Joyce and Marcel Proust, was a modernist. One goal of the modernists was to force readers to reassess their views of the novel. Philosophy and politics, as discussed by traditional intellectuals such as Mr. Ramsay, no longer had to be the dominant subject; war, epic sea voyages, and the like no longer had to be the dominant settings. As Woolf makes clear, life's intellectual, psychological, and emotional stakes can be as high in the dining room or on the lawn of one's home as they are in any boardroom or battlefield. That she later limits the discussion of World War I confirms this point.

Lily Briscoe emerges as an artist of uncompromising vision. As she stands on the lawn, trying to decide how to unite the components of the scene on her canvas, she gives the impression of being something of a bridge between Mr. and Mrs. Ramsay and the worlds they represent. Lily shares Mr. Ramsay's professional anxiety and fears that her work too will sink into oblivion—"perhaps it was better not to see pictures: they only made one hopelessly discontented with one's own work." She also possesses Mrs. Ramsay's talent for separating a moment from the passage of time and preserving it. As she watches the Ramsays move across the lawn, she invests them with a quality and meaning that make them symbolic. Later, in the last section of the novel, as Lily returns to this spot of the lawn to resume and finally complete her painting, she again serves as a vital link between Mr. and Mrs. Ramsay.

THE WINDOW: CHAPTER XVII

> [T]here is a coherence in things, a stability; something, she meant, is immune from change, and shines out. . . . (See QUOTATIONS, p. 53)

SUMMARY

Mrs. Ramsay takes her place at the dinner table and wonders what she has done with her life. As she ladles soup for her guests, she sees the true shabbiness of the room, the isolation among her guests, and the lack of beauty anywhere, and she believes herself to be responsible for fixing these problems. She again feels pity for William Bankes. Lily watches her hostess, thinking that Mrs. Ramsay looks old, worn, and remote. She senses Mrs. Ramsay's pity for Bankes and dismisses it, noting that Bankes has his work. Lily also becomes aware that she has her own work. Mrs. Ramsay asks Charles Tansley if he writes many letters, and Lily realizes that her hostess often pities men but never women. Tansley is angry at having been called away from his work and blames women for the foolishness of such gatherings. He insists again that no one will be going to the lighthouse tomorrow, and Lily reflects bitterly on Tansley's chauvinism and lack of charm. Tansley privately condemns Mrs. Ramsay for the nonsense she talks, and Lily notices his discomfort. Lily recognizes her obligation, as a woman, to comfort him, just as it would be his duty to save her from a fire in the subway. She wonders what the world would come to if men and women refused to fulfill these responsibilities. She speaks to Tansley, sarcastically asking him to take her to the lighthouse.

While Mrs. Ramsay rambles on to Tansley, William Bankes reflects on how people can grow apart, to the point that a person can be devoted to someone for whom he or she cares little. Eventually, the conversation turns to politics. Mrs. Ramsay looks to her husband, eager to hear him speak, but is disappointed to find him scowling at Augustus Carmichael, who has asked for another plate of soup. Candles are set out on the table, and they bring a change over the room, establishing a sense of order. Outside, beyond the darkened windows, the world wavers and changes. This chaos brings the guests together.

Finally having dressed for dinner, Minta Doyle and Paul Rayley take their places at the table. Minta announces that she has lost her grandmother's brooch, and Mrs. Ramsay intuits that the couple is engaged. Minta is afraid of sitting next to Mr. Ramsay, remembering his words to her about *Middlemarch,* a book she never finished reading. Meanwhile, Paul recounts the events of their walk to the beach. Dinner is served. Lily worries that she, like Paul and Minta, will need to marry, but the thought leaves her as she decides how to complete her painting. Sitting at the table, Lily notices the position of the saltshaker against the patterned tablecloth, which suggests to her something vital about the composition of her painting—the tree must be moved to the middle. Mrs. Ramsay considers that Bankes may feel some affection for her but decides that he *must* marry Lily, and she resolves to seat them closer at the next day's dinner. Everything suddenly seems possible to Mrs. Ramsay, who believes that, even in a world made of temporal things, there are qualities that endure, bringing stability and peace.

In another turn of the conversation, Bankes praises Sir Walter Scott's Waverley novels. Tansley quickly denounces this kind of reading, and Mrs. Ramsay thinks that he will be this disagreeable until he secures a professorship and a wife. She considers her children, studying Prue in particular, whom she silently promises great happiness. The guests finish dinner. Mr. Ramsay, now in great spirits, recites a poem, which Carmichael finishes as a sort of tribute to his hostess, bowing. Mrs. Ramsay leaves the room with a bow in return. On the threshold of the door, she turns back to view the scene one last time, but reflects that this special, defining moment has already become a part of the past.

ANALYSIS

The stunning scene of Mrs. Ramsay's dinner party is the heart of the novel. Here, the dominating rhythm emerges as the story moves from chaos to blissful, though momentary, order. To Mrs. Ramsay's mind, the party begins as a disaster. Minta, Paul, Andrew, and Nancy are late returning from the beach; Mr. Ramsay acts rudely toward his guests; Charles Tansley continues to bully Lily; and, although she recognizes it as her social responsibility, Lily feels ill-equipped to soothe the man's damaged ego. The opening of the chapter shifts rapidly from one partygoer's perceptions to the next, giving the impression that each person is terribly "remote"—like Tansley, they all feel "rough and isolated and lonely." But a change comes over the group as the candles are lit. Outside, the dark betrays a world in which "things wavered and vanished." The guests come together against this overwhelming uncertainty and, for the remainder of the dinner, fashion collective meaning and order out of individual existences that possess neither inherently.

At the start of the party, Mrs. Ramsay's thoughts sharply contrast with the literary allusions and learned talk of her male guests. By the end, however, she prevails in her gift, which Lily considers to be almost an artistic talent, for creating social harmony. If Mrs. Ramsay is an artist, the dinner party is her medium; indeed, if the purpose of art for her, as it is for Lily, is to break down the barriers between people, to unite and allow them to experience life together in brief, perfect understanding, then the party is nothing less than her masterpiece. The connection Lily feels between herself and Mrs. Ramsay deepens in Chapter XVII. When Lily finds herself acting out Mrs. Ramsay's behaviors toward men in her banter with Tansley, she realizes the frustrations that all women, even those in traditional roles, feel at the limitations of convention.

Despite all the tensions and imperfections evident in the Ramsay household, such as Mr. Ramsay's sometimes ridiculous vanity and Mrs. Ramsay's determination to counter the flaws in her own marriage by arranging marriages for her friends, the tone of "The Window" remains primarily bright and optimistic. The pleasant beach, the lively children, and the Ramsays' generally loving marriage suffuse the novel's world with a feeling of possibility and potential, and many of the characters have happy prospects. Paul and Minta anticipate their marriage, and Mrs. Ramsay comforts herself with her daughter Prue's future marriage as well as her son Andrew's accomplished career as a mathematician. Perhaps most important, Lily has a breakthrough that she thinks will allow her to finish her painting. With this insight comes the determination to live her life as a single woman, regardless of what Mrs. Ramsay thinks. The hope of the novel lies in Lily's resolve, for it reiterates the common bond that allows Mrs. Ramsay to have one opinion and Lily another. As the chapter closes, however, Mrs. Ramsay's realization that such harmony is always ephemeral tempers this hope. As Mrs. Ramsay leaves the room and reflects, with a glance over her shoulder, that the experience of the evening has already become part of the past, the tone of the book darkens.

The Window: Chapters XVIII–XIX

And as she looked at him she began to smile, for though she had not said a word, he knew, of course he knew, that she loved him. (See QUOTATIONS, p. 54)

Summary: Chapter XVIII

Lily contemplates the evening's disintegration once Mrs. Ramsay leaves. Some guests excuse themselves and scatter, while others remain at the table, watching Mrs. Ramsay go. The night, though over, will live on in each guest's mind, and Mrs. Ramsay is flattered to think that she too will be remembered because she was a part of the party. She goes to the nursery and discovers, to her annoyance, that the children are still awake. James and Cam sit staring at a boar's skull nailed to the wall. Cam is unable to sleep while it is there, and James refuses to allow it to be moved. Mrs. Ramsay covers it with her shawl, thus soothing both children. As Cam drifts off to sleep, James asks her if they will go to the lighthouse the next day. Mrs. Ramsay is forced to tell him no, and again, sure that he will never forget this disappointment, she feels a flash of anger toward Charles Tansley and Mr. Ramsay.

Downstairs, Prue, Minta, and Paul go to the beach to watch the waves coming in. Mrs. Ramsay wants to go with them, but she also feels an urge to stay, so she remains inside and joins her husband in the parlor.

SUMMARY: CHAPTER XIX

Mr. Ramsay sits reading a book by Sir Walter Scott. Mrs. Ramsay can tell by the controlled smile on his face that he does not wish to be disturbed, so she picks up her knitting and continues work on the stockings. She considers how insecure her husband is about his fame and worth. She is sure that he will always wonder what people think of him and his work. The poem that Mr. Ramsay and Augustus Carmichael recited during dinner returns to her. She reaches for a book of poetry. Briefly, her eyes meet her husband's. The two do not speak, though some understanding passes between them. Mr. Ramsay muses on his idea that the course of human thought is a progression from A to Z and that he is unable to move beyond Q. He thinks bitterly that it does not matter whether he ever reaches Z; someone will succeed if he fails.

After reading one of Shakespeare's sonnets, Mrs. Ramsay puts down her book and confides in her husband that Paul and Minta are engaged. Mr. Ramsay admits that he is not surprised by the news. His response leaves Mrs. Ramsay wanting more. Mr. Ramsay says that Mrs. Ramsay will not finish her stocking tonight, and she agrees. She is aware, by a sudden change of the look on his face, that he wants her to tell him that she loves him. She rarely says these words to him, and she now feels his desire to hear them. She walks to the window and looks out on the sea. She feels very beautiful and thinks that nothing on earth could match the happiness of this moment. She smiles and, though she does not say the words her husband wants to hear, she is sure that he knows. She tells him that he is right—that there will be no trip to the lighthouse the next day. He understands that these words mean that she loves him.

ANALYSIS—THE WINDOW: CHAPTERS XVIII–XIX

The harmony of the dinner party dissipates as Mr. and Mrs. Ramsay retire to the parlor to read, and the unity they feel earlier that evening disappears as they sit alone, two remote individuals reestablishing distance between them. Much of *To the Lighthouse* depends upon a rhythm that mimics the descriptions of the sea. Like a wave that rolls out and then back in again, the feeling of harmony comes and goes for the Ramsays. Their interaction in Chapter XIX is one of the most moving in the novel. In her journal, Woolf wrote that she meant *To the Lighthouse* to be such a profoundly new kind of novel that a new name would need to be found to describe the form. She suggested the word "elegy," meaning a sorrowful poem or song. There is a mournful quality to the work that gathers particular strength at the end of "The Window." Although the Ramsays share an unparalleled moment of happiness, we are keenly aware of something equally profound that will forever go unspoken between them. Given the ultimate trajectory of the novel, elegy seems a fitting description. In the second part of the novel, the ravages of time, which Mrs. Ramsay has done her best to keep at bay, descend upon the story. In this section, the symbol of the boar's skull hanging on the wall of the children's nursery prefigures this inevitable movement toward death. The juxtaposition of youth and death is a particularly potent reminder that all things, given enough time, come to the same end.

Woolf further anticipates this inevitable life cycle and, more particularly, the death of Mrs. Ramsay through her use of literary allusions. Throughout the novel, Woolf refers to other works of literature to great effect. For instance, in the opening pages Mr. Ramsay blunders through a recitation of "The Charge of the Light Brigade," which captures his anxieties about immortality, while at the dinner party the recently engaged Minta recalls Mr. Ramsay's comments about *Middlemarch*, George Eliot's novel about an unhappy marriage, whose story bears some resemblance to the trouble she later encounters with Paul. In this section, Mrs. Ramsay latches onto snatches of poetry that resonate with the larger concerns and structure of the novel. The lines from the Shakespeare sonnet that she reads, which describe the lingering presence of an absent loved one, foreshadow Mrs. Ramsay's death and continuing influence over the living. The other poem, written by Charles Elton, is titled "Luriana Lurilee." The lines that Mrs. Ramsay recites from this poem are doubly significant:

> And all the lives we ever lived
> And all the lives to be,
> Are full of trees and changing leaves.

First, the "changing leaves" confirm the larger cyclical pattern of life and death. Second, the image of the tree links Mrs. Ramsay to Lily, who believes that the success of her painting rests in moving the tree to the middle of the canvas. This connection becomes particularly important, as the hope of achieving harmony in their world comes to rest on Lily's shoulders.

TIME PASSES: CHAPTERS I–X

SUMMARY: CHAPTER I
Paul, Minta, Andrew, Prue, and Lily return from the beach. One by one, they retire to their rooms and shut off their lamps. The house sinks into darkness, except for the room of Augustus Carmichael, who stays up reading Virgil.

SUMMARY: CHAPTER II
Darkness floods the house. Furniture and people seem to disappear completely. The wind creeps indoors and is the only movement. The air plays across objects of the house—wallpaper, books, and flowers. It creeps up the stairs and continues on its way. At midnight, Carmichael blows out his candle and goes to bed.

SUMMARY: CHAPTER III
Nights pass and autumn arrives. The nights bring destructive winds, bending trees and stripping them of their leaves. Confusion reigns. Anyone who wakes to ask the night questions "as to what, and why, and wherefore" receives no answer. Mrs. Ramsay dies suddenly. The following morning, Mr. Ramsay wanders through the hallway, reaching out his arms for her.

SUMMARY: CHAPTER IV
The contents of the house are packed and stored. The winds enter and, without the resistance of lives being lived, begin to "nibble" at the possessions. As it moves across these things, the wind asks, "Will you fade? Will you perish?" The objects answer, "We

remain," and the house is peaceful. Only Mrs. McNab, the house-keeper, disturbs the peace, as she arrives to dust the bedrooms.

SUMMARY: CHAPTER V

Mrs. McNab makes her way through the house. She is old and weary and hums a tune that bears little resemblance to the joyous song of twenty years earlier. As she cleans the house, she wonders how long it all will endure. Some pleasant memory occurs to the old woman, which makes her job a bit easier.

SUMMARY: CHAPTER VI

It is spring again. Prue Ramsay marries, and people comment on her great beauty. Summer approaches, and Prue dies from an illness connected with childbirth. Flies and weeds make a home in the Ramsays' summerhouse. Andrew Ramsay is killed in France during World War I. Augustus Carmichael publishes a volume of poetry during the war that greatly enhances his reputation.

SUMMARY: CHAPTER VII

While the days bring stillness and brightness, the nights batter the house with chaos and confusion.

SUMMARY: CHAPTER VIII

Mrs. McNab, hearing a rumor that the family will never return, picks a bunch of flowers from the garden to take home with her. The house is sinking quickly into disrepair. The books are moldy and the garden is overgrown. While cleaning, the old woman comes across the gray cloak that Mrs. Ramsay used to wear while gardening, and she can imagine Mrs. Ramsay bent over her flowers with one of her children by her side. Mrs. McNab has little hope that the family will return or that the house will survive, and she thinks that keeping it up is too much work for an old woman.

SUMMARY: CHAPTER IX

During the night, only the beam of the lighthouse pierces the darkness of the house. At last, once the war is over, Mrs. McNab leads an effort to clean up the house, rescuing its objects from oblivion. She and a woman named Mrs. Bast battle the effects of time and, eventually, after much labor, get the house back in order. Ten years have passed. Lily Briscoe arrives at the house on an evening in September.

SUMMARY: CHAPTER X

Lily listens to the sea while lying in bed, and an overwhelming sense of peace emerges. Carmichael arrives at the house and reads a book by candlelight. Lily hears the waves even in her sleep, and Carmichael shuts his book, noting that everything looks much as it looked ten years earlier. The guests sleep. In the morning, Lily awakes instantly, sitting bolt upright in bed.

ANALYSIS—TIME PASSES: CHAPTERS I–X

The "Time Passes" section of *To the Lighthouse* radically alters the novel's development. Many of the characters from the first section disappear. What we learn of them in this brief following section is presented as an aside, set apart by brackets. *To the Lighthouse* frequently comments on the notion and passage of time. In "The Window," Woolf conceives of time as a matter of psychology rather than chronology. She creates what the French philosopher Henri Bergson termed *durée,* a conception of the world as primarily intuitive and internal rather than external or material. Woolf returns to this narrative strategy in the final section of the novel, "The Lighthouse." But here, in the intervening chapters, she switches gears completely and charts the relentless, cruel, and more conventional passage of time. The brackets around the deaths of Prue and Andrew associate them with Mrs. Ramsay's intermittent refrains in "The Window" and accentuate the traumatic suddenness and ultimate lack of impact these events possess. These bracketed sentences take on the tone of news bulletins or marching orders.

While "The Window" deals with the minute details of a single afternoon and evening, stretching them out into a considerable piece of prose, "Time Passes" compresses an entire decade into barely twenty pages. Woolf chooses to portray the effects of time on objects like the house and its contents rather than on human development and emotion. "Time Passes" validates Lily's and the Ramsays' fears that time will bring about their demise, as well as the widespread fear among the characters that time will erase the legacy of their work. Here, everything from the garden to the prized Waverley novels slowly sinks into oblivion.

Because the focus shifts from psychology in "The Window" to chronology in "Time Passes," human beings become secondary concerns in the latter section of the novel. This effect replicates the anxieties that plague the characters. Mr. Ramsay's fear that there is little hope for human immortality is confirmed as Woolf presents the death of the novel's heroine in an unadorned aside. This choice is remarkable on two levels. First, thematically, it skillfully asserts that human life is, in the natural scheme of things, incidental. As Mr. Ramsay notes in "The Window," a stone will outlive even Shakespeare. Second, the offhand mention of Mrs. Ramsay's death challenges established literary tradition by refusing to indulge in conventional sentiment. The emotionally hyperbolic Victorian deathbed scene is absent for Mrs. Ramsay, and Woolf uses an extreme economy of words to report the deaths of Mrs. Ramsay, Prue, and Andrew.

In this section, the darkened tone that begins to register toward the end of "The Window" comes to the fore both literally and figuratively. Mrs. Ramsay's death constitutes the death of womanhood and the dismantling of domesticated power in the novel. With the deaths of Prue and Andrew, the world's best potential and best hope seem dashed. Prue's death in childbirth strikes out at beauty and continuity, while Andrew's demise brings out the impact of war and the stunting of masculine potential so important to the novel's historical context. In a way, the novel miniaturizes a vast historical moment for Europe as a whole. "Time Passes" brings to the Ramsays destruction as vast as that inflicted on Europe by World War I. When the Ramsays return to their summer home shaken, depleted, and unsure, they represent the postwar state of an entire continent.

THE LIGHTHOUSE: CHAPTERS I–III

SUMMARY: CHAPTER I

Lily sits at breakfast, wondering what her feelings mean, returning after ten years now that Mrs. Ramsay is dead. She decides that she feels nothing that she can express. The entire scene seems unreal and disjointed to her. As she sits at the table, she struggles to bring together the parts of her experience. She suddenly remembers a painting she had been working on years ago, during her last stay at the Ramsays', and the inspiration that the leaf pattern on the tablecloth gave her. She decides that she will finish this painting now, heads outside, and sets up her easel on the lawn. Upon her arrival the previous night, she was unable to assuage Mr. Ramsay's need for sympathy, and she fears his interference with her current project. She sets a clean canvas on the easel, but she cannot see the shapes or colors that surround her because she feels Mr. Ramsay bearing down on her. She thinks angrily that all Mr. Ramsay knows how to do is take, while all Mrs. Ramsay did was give. As her host approaches, Lily lets her brush fall to her side, convinced that it will be easier to remember and imitate the sympathy that Mrs. Ramsay was able to muster for her husband than to let him linger on the lawn beside her.

Summary: Chapter II

Mr. Ramsay watches Lily, observing her to be "shrivelled slightly" but not unattractive. He asks if she has everything she needs, and she assures him that she does. Lily cannot give him the sympathy he needs, and an awful silence falls between them. Mr. Ramsay sighs, waiting. Lily feels that, as a woman, she is a failure for not being able to satisfy his need. Eventually, she compliments him on his boots, and he gladly discusses footwear with her. He stoops to demonstrate the proper way to tie a shoe, and she pities him deeply. Just then, Cam and James appear for the sojourn to the lighthouse. They are cold and unpleasant to their father, and Lily reflects that, if they so wished, they could sympathize with him in a way that she cannot.

Summary: Chapter III

Lily sighs with relief as Mr. Ramsay and the children head off for the boat. With Mr. Ramsay standing by, she had jammed her easel into the ground at the wrong angle and taken up the wrong brush. She rights the canvas, raises the correct brush, and wonders where to begin. She makes a stroke on the canvas, then another. Her painting takes on a rhythm, as she dabs and pauses, dabs and pauses. She considers the fate of her painting, thinking that if it is to be hung in a servant's room or rolled up under a sofa, there is no point in continuing it. The derogatory words of Charles Tansley—that women cannot paint, cannot write—return to her, but she maintains the rhythm of her work. She remembers a day on the beach with Tansley and Mrs. Ramsay, and is amazed by Mrs. Ramsay's ability to craft substance out of even "silliness and spite." She thinks, perhaps, that there are no great revelations. There is, to her, only the memory of Mrs. Ramsay making life itself an art. Lily feels that she owes what revelation she has in this moment to Mrs. Ramsay. On the edge of the water, she notices a boat with its sail being hoisted and, sure that it belongs to the Ramsays, watches it head out to sea.

ANALYSIS—THE LIGHTHOUSE: CHAPTERS I–III

The structure of *To the Lighthouse* creates a strange feeling of continuity between drastically discontinuous events. "The Window" ends after dinner, as night falls; "Time Passes" describes the demise of the house as one night passes into the next over the course of ten years; "The Lighthouse" resumes in the morning, at breakfast. Woolf almost suggests the illusion that Lily sits at the table the morning after the dinner party, even though the scene takes place a decade later. This structure lends the impression that Mr. Ramsay's voyage to the lighthouse with Cam and James occurs the next day as James had hoped, though his world is now wholly different.

In spite of these differences, the Ramsays' house in the Hebrides remains recognizable, as do the rhythmic patterns of the characters' consciousnesses. As Woolf resumes her exploration of the subtle undercurrents of interpersonal relationships, she begins with characters who are "remote" from one another. They occupy, in fact, the same positions of private suffering as at the beginning of Mrs. Ramsay's magnificent dinner party. Mr. Ramsay, a man in decline, is no longer imposing to Lily. Rather, he is awkward and pathetic. His children are waging a barely veiled revolt against his oppressive and self-pitying behavior. Still desperate for sympathy but unable to obtain it from Mrs. Ramsay, Mr. Ramsay turns to Lily and his children to satisfy his need. Lily, on the other hand, still feels unable to give of herself in this way. Her reluctance to show sympathy to Mr. Ramsay recalls her reaction to Charles Tansley at the dinner table. Then, as now, she cannot bring herself to soothe the tortured male ego. The world, as a result of these disjointed personalities and desires, seems "chaotic" and "aimless," and Lily concludes that the house is brimming with "unrelated passions."

"The Window" establishes a rhythm between chaos and order, which allows us to anticipate the direction that "The Lighthouse" will take. Mr. Ramsay eventually reaches the lighthouse, just as Lily eventually completes her painting. The poignant scene in which Mr. Ramsay bends to knot Lily's shoe foreshadows the "common feeling" that the two share when Lily's consciousness becomes tied to her host's. Before this union can happen, though, the two must be separated. Indeed, Lily's thoughts toward Mr. Ramsay begin to soften only after he leaves her alone at her easel and sets off for the lighthouse. Only then does the sight of Cam, James, and Mr. Ramsay reveal itself as a potential image of harmony—"a little company bound together and strangely impressive to her."

Memory is another vital step toward this harmony. Though long dead, Mrs. Ramsay lives in Lily's consciousness in the final section of the novel, for it was Mrs. Ramsay who taught Lily a valuable lesson about the nature of art. As her hostess once demonstrated on an outing to the beach, art is the ability to take a moment from life and make it "permanent." With this goal in mind, Lily begins to paint.

THE LIGHTHOUSE: CHAPTERS IV–VII

SUMMARY: CHAPTER IV

As the boat sails toward the lighthouse, both James and Cam feel their father's mounting anxiety and impatience. Mr. Ramsay mutters and speaks sharply to Macalister's boy, a fisherman's son who is rowing the boat. Bound together against what they perceive to be their father's tyranny, the children resolve to make the journey in silence. They secretly hope that the wind will never rise and that they will be forced to turn back. But as they sail farther out, the sails pick up the wind and the boat speeds along. James steers the boat and mans the sail, knowing that his father will criticize him if he makes the slightest mistake.

Mr. Ramsay talks to Macalister about a storm that sank a number of ships near the lighthouse on Christmas. Cam realizes that her father likes to hear stories of men having dangerous adventures and thinks that he would have helped the rescue effort had he been on the island at the time. She is proud of him, but also, out of loyalty to James, means to resist his oppressive behavior. Mr. Ramsay points out their house, and Cam reflects how unreal life on shore seems. Only the boat and the sea are real to her now. Cam, though disgusted by her father's melodramatic appeals for sympathy, longs to find a way to show him that she loves him without betraying James. James, for his part, feels that Cam is about to abandon him and give in to their father's mood. Meanwhile, Mr. Ramsay muses that Cam seems to have a simple, vague "female" mind, which he finds charming. He asks Cam who is looking after their puppy, and she tells him that Jasper is doing it. He asks what she is going to name the puppy, and James thinks that Cam will never withstand their father's tyranny like he will. He changes his mind about her resolve, however, and Cam thinks of how everything she hears her father say means "Submit to me." She looks at the shore, thinking no one suffers there.

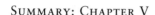

SUMMARY: CHAPTER V

Lily stands on the lawn watching the boat sail off. She thinks again of Mrs. Ramsay as she considers her painting. She thinks of Paul and Minta Rayley and contents herself by imagining their lives. Their marriage, she assumes, turned out badly. Though she knows that these sorts of imaginings are not true, she reflects that they are what allow one to know people. Lily has the urge to share her stories of Paul and Minta with the matchmaking Mrs. Ramsay, and reflects on the dead, contending that one can go against their wishes and improve on their outdated ideas. She finally feels able to stand up to Mrs. Ramsay, which, she believes, is a testament to Mrs. Ramsay's terrific influence over her. Lily has never married, and she is glad of it now. She still enjoys William Bankes's friendship and their discussions about art. The memory of Mrs. Ramsay fills her with grief, and she begins to cry. She has the urge to approach Augustus Carmichael, who lounges nearby on the lawn, and confess her thoughts to him, but she knows that she could never say what she means.

SUMMARY: CHAPTER VI

The fisherman's boy cuts a piece from a fish that he has caught and baits it on his hook. He then throws the mutilated body into the sea.

SUMMARY: CHAPTER VII

Lily calls out to Mrs. Ramsay as if the woman might return, but nothing happens. She hopes that her cries will heal her pain, but is glad that Carmichael does not hear them. Eventually, the anguish subsides, and Lily returns to her painting, working on her representation of the hedge. She imagines Mrs. Ramsay, radiant with beauty and crowned with flowers, walking across the lawn. The image soothes her. She notices a boat in the middle of the bay and wonders if it is the Ramsays'.

ANALYSIS—THE LIGHTHOUSE: CHAPTERS IV–VII

Although Chapter VI is presented in brackets and is only two sentences long, its description of a live mutilated fish is important to the novel since the fish represents the paradox of the world as an extremely cruel place in which survival is somehow possible. The brackets also hearken back to the reports of violence and sorrow in "Time Passes," which recount the deaths of Prue and Andrew Ramsay. *To the Lighthouse* is filled with symbols that have no easily assigned meaning. The mutilated fish, the boar's head wrapped in Mrs. Ramsay's shawl, Lily's painting, and the lighthouse itself are symbols that require us to sift through a multiplicity of meanings rather than pin down a single interpretation.

Mrs. Ramsay and the pasts of her guests and children haunt the novel's final section. As Lily stands on the lawn watching the Ramsays' boat move out into the bay, she is possessed by thoughts of Mrs. Ramsay, while Macalister spins out stories of shipwrecks and drowned sailors, and Cam reflects that there is no suffering on the distant shore where people are "free to come and go like ghosts." At first, Mrs. Ramsay exerts her old pull on Lily, who begins to feel anxious about the choices she has made in life. But as her thoughts turn to Paul and Minta Rayley, around whom she has built up "a whole structure of imagination," Lily begins to exorcise Mrs. Ramsay's spirit and better understand her old friend. Though she readily admits in regard to her imagining of the Rayleys' failed marriage that "not a word of it [is] true," she believes that her version of their lives constitutes real knowledge of the couple; thus, the novel again insists upon the subjective nature of reality. These thoughts allow Lily to approach Mrs. Ramsay, who insisted on Paul's marriage, from a new, more critical, and ultimately more truthful angle.

Lily's longing for Mrs. Ramsay is a result of understanding her as a more complicated, flawed individual. When she wakes that morning, Lily reflects solemnly that Mrs. Ramsay's absence at the breakfast table evokes no particular feelings in her; now, however, Lily calls out Mrs. Ramsay's name, as if attempting to chant her back from the grave. Lily's anguish and dissonance force us to reassess her art. Mrs. Ramsay's beauty has always rendered Lily speechless, but Lily now realizes that "[b]eauty had this penalty—it came too readily, came too completely. It stilled life—froze it." She mimics Mrs. Ramsay's psychological gesture of smoothing away life's complexities and flaws under a veneer of beauty. Continuing to paint, Lily feels a deeper need to locate the Ramsays' boat on the water and reach out to Mr. Ramsay, to whom a short while earlier she feels that she has nothing to give.

THE LIGHTHOUSE: CHAPTERS VIII–XIII

> *No, the other was also the Lighthouse. For nothing was simply one thing. The other Lighthouse was true too.* (See QUOTATIONS, p. 55)

SUMMARY: CHAPTER VIII

"They don't feel a thing there," Cam muses to herself while looking at the shore. Her mind moves in swirls and waves like the sea, until the wind slows and the boat comes to a stop between the lighthouse and the shore. Mr. Ramsay sits in the boat reading a book, and James waits with dread for the moment that his father will turn to him with some criticism. James realizes that he now hates and wants to kill not his father but the moods that descend on his father. He likens the dark sarcasm that makes his father intolerable to a wheel that runs over a foot and crushes it. In other words, Mr. Ramsay is as much a victim of these spells of tyranny as James and Cam. He remembers his father telling him years ago that he would not be able to go to the lighthouse. Then, the lighthouse was silvery and misty; now, when he is much closer to it, it looks starker. James is astonished at how little his present view of the scene resembles his former image of it, but he reflects that nothing is ever only one thing; both images of the lighthouse are true. He remembers his mother, who left him sitting with the Army and Navy Stores catalogue after Mr. Ramsay dismissed their initial trip to the lighthouse. Mrs. Ramsay remains a source of "everlasting attraction" to James, for he believes she spoke the truth and said exactly what came into her head.

SUMMARY: CHAPTER IX

Lily watches the sea. She notes the power of distance and how it has swallowed the Ramsays and herself. All is calm and quiet. A steamship disappears from sight, though its smoke lingers in the air.

SUMMARY: CHAPTER X

Cam feels liberated from her father's anger and her brother's expectations. She feels overjoyed at having escaped the burden of these things, and entertains herself with a story of adventure. She imagines herself escaping from a sinking ship. She wonders what place the distant island has in the grand scheme of things and is certain that her father and the men with whom he keeps company (such as

William Bankes and Augustus Carmichael) could tell her. She feels incredibly safe in her father's presence and wishes her brother would put aside his grievances with him.

Summary: Chapter XI

Back on shore, Lily loses herself in her intense memories of Mrs. Ramsay, noticing Carmichael when he grunts and picks up his book and reflecting on the freedom from conventional chatter the early morning hour provides. Watching the sailboat approach the lighthouse, she contemplates distance as crucially important to one's understanding of other people. As Mr. Ramsay recedes into the horizon, he begins to seem to her a different person altogether.

Similarly, Lily's understanding of Mrs. Ramsay has changed considerably since Mrs. Ramsay's death. Lily thinks about the people she once knew at this house, about Carmichael's poetry, about Charles Tansley's marriage, his career in academics, and his educating his little sister. She recalls having heard Tansley denounce the war and advocate brotherly love, which did not fit her understanding of him at all. But she thinks that people interpret one another in ways that reflect their own needs. To see someone clearly and fully, she concludes, one would need more than fifty pairs of eyes. Lily thinks about the Ramsays' marriage, saying that theirs did not constitute marital bliss. She recounts to herself the domestic forces that occupied and tired Mrs. Ramsay, then notices what looks like a figure in the window of the house. The image is fleeting, however, and leaves Lily yearning for Mrs. Ramsay and wishing that Mr. Ramsay would return.

Summary: Chapter XII

Mr. Ramsay is almost finished with his book. The sight of the lighthouse inspires James to recognize the profound loneliness that both he and his father feel. James mutters a snatch of poetry under his breath, as Mr. Ramsay often does. Cam stares at the sea and becomes sleepy. James steers the boat, and Mr. Ramsay opens their parcel of food and they eat. The fisherman says that three men drowned in the spot the boat is in. Mr. Ramsay reiterates the line of verse, "But I beneath a rougher sea." James lands the boat, and Mr. Ramsay praises James's sailing. Cam thinks that James has gotten what he has always wanted—his father's praise—but James, unwilling to share his pleasure, acts sullen and indifferent. As Mr. Ramsay stands and looks at the lighthouse, Cam wonders what he sees, what

SUMMARY & ANALYSIS

he thinks. He tells his children to bring the parcels that Nancy has packed for the voyage and bounds, like a young man, onto the rock.

SUMMARY: CHAPTER XIII

On the shore, Lily declares aloud that her painting is finished, and notes that Mr. Ramsay must have reached the lighthouse by now. Carmichael rises up and looks at the sea, agreeing that the sailboat must have reached its destination. Lily draws a final line on her painting and realizes that it is truly finished, feeling a weary sense of relief. She realizes that she does not care whether it will be hung in attics or destroyed, for she has had her vision.

ANALYSIS — THE LIGHTHOUSE: CHAPTERS VIII–XIII

James's reflection on the lighthouse underlines the contradictory psychological and narrative structures of the book. The lighthouse provides James with a chance to consider the subjective nature of his consciousness. He decides that the tower can be two competing images at once: it is, for him, both a relic of his childhood fantasy *and* the stark, brutally real and somewhat banal structure he now sees before him. Just as Lily concludes that she would need more than fifty pairs of eyes in order to gain a complete picture of Mrs. Ramsay, James realizes that nothing is ever only one thing—the world is far too complex for such reduction and simplification. These metaphors explain Woolf's technique. Only by presenting the narrative as a collection of varied and competing consciousnesses could she hope to capture a true likeness of her characters and their worlds.

In the final pages of the novel, Woolf reveals the key to the reconciliation of competing impressions that allows James to view the lighthouse and Lily to see Mrs. Ramsay in the context of both the past and present. This key is distance, which Lily notes in Chapter IX has "extraordinary power." Lily has had ten years to process her thoughts regarding Mrs. Ramsay, ten years to work her way beyond an influence that, in the opening pages of the novel, overwhelms her with its intensity. When, earlier, Lily sits at Mrs. Ramsay's feet, she is blinded by her love for the woman. Her opinion of Mrs. Ramsay has changed considerably by the end of the novel. She recognizes Mrs. Ramsay's dated ways and somewhat manipulative nature, and her vision of Mrs. Ramsay is now more complete. Likewise, James is better able to see the lighthouse and, more pivotal, his father because of the distance that separates him from his childhood impressions. Mr. Ramsay, as Cam realizes, is not the same man he was ten years ago. Although still domineering, he has become more sensitive, a fact that James, overjoyed with the compliment his father has paid him, might finally begin to see.

Woolf's phrasing of Lily's declaration of "[i]t is finished" lends gravity and power to the moment with its biblical echoes of death and impending rebirth. The moment also parallels James's ability to see the lighthouse and his father anew but holds singular importance for the structure of the novel. Mr. Ramsay, Mrs. Ramsay, and Lily Briscoe make three distinct attempts to harness the chaos that is life and make it meaningful. As a philosopher, Mr. Ramsay fails to progress to the end of human thought, that elusive letter Z that he believes represents the ultimate knowledge of life, while Mrs. Ramsay dies before she sees her children married. Thus, both the intellectual and social attempts to order life fall short. Only Lily's attempt at artistic order succeeds, and it does so with grace and power. Lily has a "vision" that enables her to bring the separate, conflicting objects of her composition into harmony. This synthesizing impulse counters the narrative fragmentation as well as the competing worldviews among the characters. The painting represents a single instant lifted out of the flow of time and made permanent.

IMPORTANT QUOTATIONS EXPLAINED

1.   Who shall blame him? Who will not secretly rejoice
     when the hero puts his armour off, and halts by the
     window and gazes at his wife and son, who, very
     distant at first, gradually come closer and closer, till
     lips and book and head are clearly before him, though
     still lovely and unfamiliar from the intensity of his
     isolation and the waste of ages and the perishing of
     the stars, and finally putting his pipe in his pocket and
     bending his magnificent head before her—who will
     blame him if he does homage to the beauty of
     the world?

As Mr. Ramsay strolls across the lawn in Chapter VI of "The Window," he catches sight of Mrs. Ramsay and James in the window.
His reaction comes as something of a surprise given the troubled
ruminations of his mind described just pages before. He, like nearly
every character in the novel, is keenly aware of the inevitability of
death and the likelihood of its casting his existence into absolute
oblivion. Mr. Ramsay knows that few men achieve intellectual
immortality. The above passage testifies to his knowledge that all
things, from the stars in the sky to the fruits of his career, are
doomed to perish. Here, rather than cave in to the anxieties brought
on by that knowledge, punish James for dreaming of the lighthouse,
or demand that Mrs. Ramsay or Lily lavish him with sympathy, Mr.
Ramsay satisfies himself by appreciating the beauty that surrounds
him. The tableau of his wife and child cannot last—after all, they
will eventually move and break the pose—but it has the power, nevertheless, to assuage his troubled mind. These moments integrate
the random fragments of experience and interaction in the world.
As Mr. Ramsay brings his wife and son visually "closer and closer,"
the distance among the three shortens, buoying Mr. Ramsay up
from the depths of despair.

2. Could loving, as people called it, make her and Mrs.
    Ramsay one? for it was not knowledge but unity that
    she desired, not inscriptions on tablets, nothing that
    could be written in any language known to men, but
    intimacy itself, which is knowledge, she had thought,
    leaning her head on Mrs. Ramsay's knee.

These musings come from Lily in Chapter IX of "The Window," as
she and William Bankes stand on the lawn watching the Ramsays.
Bankes criticizes Mr. Ramsay for his hypocrisy in being narrow-
minded, and Lily is about to respond with a criticism of Mrs.
Ramsay when she notices the look of rapture on Bankes's face. She
realizes that he loves Mrs. Ramsay, and she feels that this emotion is
a contribution to the good of humanity. Overwhelmed with love
herself, Lily approaches Mrs. Ramsay and sits beside her. Her
thoughts here are noteworthy because they point to the distinction
between ways of acquiring knowledge: instinct, on the one hand,
and intelligence, on the other. Mrs. Ramsay knows what she does of
the world by the former method, while Mr. Ramsay depends upon
"inscriptions on tablets." Here, as she wonders how one person
comes to truly know another, Lily straddles the line that separates
emotions from intellect, and that separates Mrs. Ramsay from her
husband. This position anticipates Lily's role at the end of the novel,
when she stands watching Mr. Ramsay's boat and indulges in powerful remembrances of Mrs. Ramsay. At that moment, Lily arrives
at her elusive vision, completes her painting, and achieves the unity
she craves in the above passage.

3.   It partook . . . of eternity . . . there is a coherence in
     things, a stability; something, she meant, is immune
     from change, and shines out (she glanced at the
     window with its ripple of reflected lights) in the face
     of the flowing, the fleeting, the spectral, like a ruby; so
     that again tonight she had the feeling she had had
     once today, already, of peace, of rest. Of such
     moments, she thought, the thing is made that endures.

Chapter XVII of "The Window" is, in many respects, the heart of
the novel. In Mrs. Ramsay's dinner party, we see the rhythmic
movement from chaos to order, from obscurity to clarity of vision,
through which the novel progresses. The dinner party begins, to
Mrs. Ramsay's mind, as something of a disaster. Not all of the
guests have arrived (Paul and Minta, for instance, have yet to return
from the beach with Andrew and Nancy); Charles Tansley makes
hostile comments to Lily; Augustus Carmichael offends his host by
asking for a second plate of soup. Soon enough, however, as darkness descends outside and the candles are lit, the evening rights
itself. Everyone is content, as Mrs. Ramsay intends, and everyone
will remember the evening as beautiful and right. This passage
describes these rare, priceless moments, which take on a kind of psychological permanence. The guests will remember this evening and
will experience, with inexorable nostalgia, peace, and rest. In a
world in which struggle and destruction are inevitable, the possibility for such domestic respite provides great comfort.

QUOTATIONS

4. [S]he could not say it. . . . [A}s she looked at him she
    began to smile, for though she had not said a word, he
    knew, of course he knew, that she loved him. He
    could not deny it. And smiling she looked out of the
    window and said (thinking to herself, Nothing on
    earth can equal this happiness)—

      "Yes, you were right. It's going to be wet
    tomorrow. You won't be able to go." And she looked
    at him smiling. For she had triumphed again. She had
    not said it: yet he knew.

This passage, taken from Chapter XIX of "The Window," is a lyri-
cal demonstration of how disjointed people and their fragmented
emotions can come together. Mr. and Mrs. Ramsay represent opposite approaches to life. Possessed of a stolidly rational and scientific
mind, Mr. Ramsay relies on what can be studied, proven, and spo-
ken. Hence, at the end of "The Window," he wants to hear Mrs.
Ramsay declare her love for him. Mrs. Ramsay, however, navigates
life on a less predictable course. She is led by her emotions rather
than her mind. This approach provides her a greater range and freedom of expression. For instance, she can express her affection for
her guests by orchestrating a lovely and memorable evening rather
than forcing herself to articulate (or, like Mr. Ramsay, punish herself for not being able to articulate) these feelings. In Woolf's estima-
tion, these traits are gender-specific. She argues that men are most
often satisfied by direct declarations, as when, in the novel's final
pages, James is mollified only by his father's praise of his sailing
skills. Women, on the other hand, often convey their meaning by
what they choose *not* to say. Like Mrs. Ramsay in her triumph at the
end of "The Window," Lily is able to convey her sympathy for Mr.
Ramsay without pronouncing it: she lets him tie her shoe.

5. The Lighthouse was then a silvery, misty-looking
tower with a yellow eye, that opened suddenly, and
softly in the evening. Now—
James looked at the Lighthouse. He could see the
white-washed rocks; the tower, stark and straight; he
could see that it was barred with black and white; he
could see windows in it; he could even see washing
spread on the rocks to dry. So that was the
Lighthouse, was it?
No, the other was also the Lighthouse. For nothing
was simply one thing. The other Lighthouse was
true too.

As the Ramsays' boat approaches the lighthouse in Chapter VIII of
"The Lighthouse," James reflects on images of the edifice that are
competing in his mind. The first is from his childhood, when the
lighthouse, seen from a distance, was a "silvery, misty-looking
tower." The second image, formed as he sails closer, is stripped of its
shadows and romance. The structure appears hard, plain, and real.
Its barred windows and the laundry drying on the rocks present
nothing magical. James's first inclination is to banish one of these
pictures from his mind and grant the other sovereignty, but he cor-
rects himself, realizing that the lighthouse is both what it was then
and what it is now. The task that James faces is a reconciliation of
these competing images into a whole truth. This challenge is the
same one that Lily faces at the end of the novel, for she must reconcile her romantic vision of, and disappointment with, Mrs. Ramsay.
To do so and to admit the complex, even contradictory, nature of all
things, the novel suggests, is to possess a greater (and more artful)
understanding of life.

QUOTATIONS

KEY FACTS

FULL TITLE
To the Lighthouse

AUTHOR
Virginia Woolf

TYPE OF WORK
Novel

GENRE
Stream of consciousness

LANGUAGE
English

TIME AND PLACE WRITTEN
1926, London

DATE OF FIRST PUBLICATION
1927

PUBLISHER
Hogarth Press

NARRATOR
The narrator is anonymous.

POINT OF VIEW
The narrator speaks in the third person and describes the
characters and actions subjectively, giving us insight into the
characters' feelings. The narrative switches constantly from the
perceptions of one character to those of the next.

TONE
Elegiac, poetic, rhythmic, imaginative

TENSE
Past

SETTING (TIME)
The years immediately preceding and following World War I

SETTING (PLACE)

The Isle of Skye, in the Hebrides (a group of islands west of Scotland)

PROTAGONIST

Although Mrs. Ramsay is the central focus of the beginning of *To the Lighthouse,* the novel traces the development of Lily Briscoe to the end, making it more accurate to describe Lily as the protagonist.

MAJOR CONFLICT

The common struggle that each of the characters faces is to bring meaning and order to the chaos of life.

RISING ACTION

James's desire to journey to the lighthouse; Mr. Ramsay's need to ask Mrs. Ramsay for sympathy; Charles Tansley's insistence that women cannot paint or write; Lily Briscoe's stalled attempt at her painting

CLIMAX

Mrs. Ramsay's dinner party

FALLING ACTION

Mr. Ramsay's trip to the lighthouse with Cam and James; Lily Briscoe's completion of her painting

THEMES

The transience of life and work; art as a means of preservation; the subjective nature of reality; the restorative effects of beauty

MOTIFS

The differing behaviors of men and women; brackets

SYMBOLS

The lighthouse, Lily's painting, the Ramsays' house, the sea, the boar's skull, the fruit basket

FORESHADOWING

James's initial desire and anxiety surrounding the voyage to the lighthouse foreshadows the trip he makes a decade later.

Study Questions & Essay Topics

Study Questions

1. *What are some of the main symbols in* To the Lighthouse, *and what do they signify? How does Woolf's use of symbolism advance her thematic goals?*

James gives us a clue as to how to interpret symbols in *To the Lighthouse*. As he finally draws the Ramsays' boat up to the lighthouse, he considers two competing, and seemingly contradictory, meanings of the lighthouse. The first depends upon the lighthouse as it appeared to him as a child; then, it was a "silvery, mist-colored tower" and seemed to suggest the vague, romantic quality of the past. The second meaning stands in opposition, for, as James nears the lighthouse and sees its barred windows and laundry drying on the rocks, there is nothing romantic about it. He resolves, however, to honor the truth of both images, deciding that "nothing [is] simply one thing."

Like James's interpretation of the lighthouse, the dominant symbols in the novel demand open readings. Mrs. Ramsay wrapping her shawl around the boar's head can be read merely as protection of her impressionable children from the unsightly suggestion of death, but it can also be read as a selfish attempt to keep from them a profound and inescapable truth. Choosing one option or the other diminishes the complexity of the novel's symbols and characters. Woolf resists formulaic symbols, whereby one entity straightforwardly stands for another; she thus places us in the same position as her characters. The world of the novel is not filled with solidly or surely determined truths. Rather, truth, as Lily points out, must be collected from an endless number of impressions—she wishes that she had more than fifty pairs of eyes with which to view Mrs. Ramsay and understand her. We must approach the symbolism of *To the Lighthouse* with the same patience for multiple meanings.

2. *If* To the Lighthouse *is a novel about the search for meaning in life, how do the characters conduct their search? Are they successful in finding an answer?*

Although all the characters engage themselves in the same quest for meaningful experience, the three main characters have vastly different approaches. Mr. Ramsay's search is intellectual; he hopes to understand the world and his place in it by working at philosophy and reading books. Mrs. Ramsay conducts her search through intuition rather than intellect; she relies on social traditions such as marriage and dinner parties to structure her experience. Lily, on the other hand, tries to create meaning in her life through her painting; she seeks to unify disparate elements in a harmonious whole.

While these characters experience varying degrees of success in their quest for meaning, none arrives at a revelation that fulfills the search. As an old man, Mr. Ramsay continues to be as tortured by the specter of his own mortality as he is in youth. Mrs. Ramsay achieves moments in which life seems filled with meaning, but, as her dinner party makes clear, they are terribly short-lived. Lily, too, manages to wrest a moment from life and lend to it meaning and order. Her painting is a small testament to that struggle. But, as she reflects while pondering the meaning of her life, there are no "great revelations" but only "little daily miracles" that one, if lucky, can fish out of the dark.

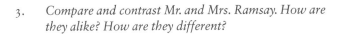

3.   *Compare and contrast Mr. and Mrs. Ramsay. How are*
     they alike? How are they different?

Although Mr. and Mrs. Ramsay's love for each other and for their children is beyond doubt, their approaches to life could not be more opposite. Mrs. Ramsay is loving, kind to her children, selfless, and generously giving, while Mr. Ramsay is cold and socially awkward. He is stern with his children, which causes them to hate and fear him, and he displays a neediness that makes him rather pathetic in the eyes of his guests. Despite these profound differences, however, Mr. and Mrs. Ramsay share the knowledge that all things—from human life to human happiness—are destined to end. It is from this shared knowledge that their greatest differences grow. Keenly aware of human mortality, Mrs. Ramsay is fueled to cultivate moments that soothe her consciousness, while Mr. Ramsay nearly collapses under the weight of this realization.

SUGGESTED ESSAY TOPICS

1. *To the Lighthouse* opens with a portrayal of the Oedipal struggle between James and Mr. Ramsay. This conflict resounds throughout the book. How does the family drama shape the book as a whole?

2. Conventional gender roles—and more broadly, conventional social roles—present a major subject of exploration in *To the Lighthouse.* Choose three characters and describe how each approaches this subject. Do gender roles play a part in the lives of the younger children?

3. What effect does the ocean have on different characters at different times in the novel? Why, for example, do the waves make Mrs. Ramsay sad?

4. What makes the "Time Passes" section so different from the rest of the novel? Why do you think Woolf chose such an unusual narrative approach for this section?

5. How does work function in the novel? For example, how does Lily approach what she sees as her work? How do Mr. Ramsay and Charles Tansley approach what they see as their work?

REVIEW & RESOURCES

QUIZ

1. What will outlive the memory of Shakespeare, according to Mr. Ramsay?

    A. A small stone
    B. A grain of sand
    C. Titian's oil paintings
    D. His love for Mrs. Ramsay

2. As the novel begins, how does young James Ramsay occupy himself?

    A. He stares out the window at the lighthouse
    B. He hunts rabbits
    C. He clips pictures from the Army and Navy Stores catalogue
    D. He plays with the skull that hangs on the nursery wall

3. To whom does Lily show her painting?

    A. Mrs. Ramsay
    B. William Bankes
    C. Mr. Ramsay
    D. Charles Tansley

4. How does Andrew Ramsay die?

    A. He is shot by Jasper
    B. He falls from a train
    C. He catches typhoid fever
    D. He is killed in World War I

5. To what does Mr. Ramsay liken the progress of human thought?

    A. An alphabet
    B. An abacus
    C. A long, dark road
    D. A lighthouse

6. Who originally asks to go to the lighthouse?

    A. Prue
    B. Andrew
    C. James
    D. Nancy

7. Why does Paul Rayley feel dissatisfied by his marriage proposal?

    A. He stumbled over the words
    B. He feels tricked by Mrs. Ramsay
    C. Minta refused him
    D. Minta said yes to him but refused to kiss him

8. What article of clothing does Mrs. Ramsay make for the lighthouse keeper's son?

    A. A shirt
    B. Long underwear
    C. Trousers
    D. A stocking

9. How did Virginia Woolf die?

    A. She drowned herself
    B. She had a fatal stroke
    C. She had a heart attack
    D. She died in a car accident

10. Who tells Lily that women can never paint or write?

    A. Mr. Ramsay
    B. Charles Tansley
    C. James
    D. Mrs. Ramsay

11. What poem does Mr. Ramsay recite to himself on the beach?

    A. "Dover Beach"
    B. "The Collar"
    C. "The Charge of the Light Brigade"
    D. "Maud"

12. Who chooses Mrs. Ramsay's jewelry for the dinner party?

    A. Emily
    B. Rose
    C. Mabel
    D. Clarissa

13. What was the name of the group of artists and intellectuals to which Woolf belonged?

    A. The Bloomsbury Group
    B. The Soho Group
    C. The Magdaleners
    D. The Whiteacres

14. In what year was *To the Lighthouse* published?

    A. 1882
    B. 1905
    C. 1927
    D. 1941

15. Which character does Mrs. Ramsay hope Lily will marry?

    A. Charles Tansley
    B. Augustus Carmichael
    C. Andrew
    D. William Bankes

16. What revives interest in Mr. Carmichael's poetry?

    A. His reading of a poem on BBC radio
    B. His new volume of poems published during World War I
    C. His trial
    D. His death

17.   How does Prue Ramsay die?

    A.   She is a civilian casualty of the war
    B.   She is stricken by cancer
    C.   She is stricken by an illness related to childbirth
    D.   She falls from a train

18.   What does Mr. Ramsay most often want from Mrs. Ramsay and why?

    A.   Sympathy; he is full of professional anxiety
    B.   Food; he has an enormous appetite and she is a masterful cook
    C.   Money; he is lazy and spends lavishly
    D.   Advice; he trusts Mrs. Ramsay to guide his career

19.   Critical consensus holds that the character of Mrs. Ramsay is based on whom?

    A.   Woolf's sister
    B.   Woolf's friend Clarissa, from Cambridge
    C.   Vita Sackville-West
    D.   Woolf's mother

20.   Who accompanies Mr. Ramsay to the lighthouse at the novel's end?

    A.   James and Mrs. Ramsay
    B.   James and Cam
    C.   Minta Doyle and Paul Rayley
    D.   James and Lily Briscoe

21.   How many years pass in the second section of the novel?

    A.   5
    B.   10
    C.   12
    D.   20

22. Who rescues the house from the disastrous effects of time?

    A. Mrs. Ramsay
    B. Mr. Ramsay
    C. Mrs. McNab
    D. Mr. Macalister

23. What does Mrs. Ramsay read when she joins Mr. Ramsay after the dinner party?

    A. A Shakespearean sonnet
    B. The Army and Navy Stores catalogue
    C. The daily newspaper
    D. A novel by Sir Walter Scott

24. What does Minta Doyle lose on the beach?

    A. The engagement ring that Paul gave her
    B. James's favorite seashell
    C. A rare coin
    D. Her grandmother's brooch

25. When Mrs. Ramsay discovers the children awake in the nursery, what does she do to help them sleep?

    A. She sings a lullaby
    B. She mixes sleeping powder in their milk
    C. She covers a skull that hangs on the wall with her shawl
    D. She uses the stocking she has been knitting to give a puppet show

ANSWER KEY:

1: A; 2: C; 3: B; 4: D; 5: A; 6: C; 7: B; 8: D; 9: A; 10: B;
11: C; 12: B; 13: A; 14: C; 15: D; 16: B; 17: C; 18: A; 19: D;
20: B; 21: B; 22: C; 23: A; 24: D; 25: C

SUGGESTIONS FOR FURTHER READING

BEJA, MORRIS, ed. TO THE LIGHTHOUSE: *A Casebook*. London: Macmillan, 1970.

DE GAY, JANE. "Behind the Purple Triangle: Art and Iconography in *To the Lighthouse*." *Woolf Studies Annual* 5 (1999): 1-23.

HYMAN, VIRGINIA R. TO THE LIGHTHOUSE *and Beyond: Transformations in the Narratives of Virginia Woolf*. New York: P. Lang, 1988.

INGRAM, PENELOPE. "'One Drifts Apart': *To the Lighthouse* as Art of Response." *Philosophy and Literature* 23, no. 1 (1999): 78-95.

KATO, MEGUMI. "The Politics/Poetics of Motherhood in *To the Lighthouse* In *Virginia Woolf and Communities,* ed. Laura Davis and Jeanette McVicker. New York: Pace University Press, 1999.

KELLEY, ALICE VAN BUREN. TO THE LIGHTHOUSE: *The Marriage of Life and Art*. Boston: Twayne Publishers, 1987.

KNOX-SHAW, PETER. "*To the Lighthouse*: The Novel as Elegy." *English Studies in Africa: A Journal of the Humanities* 29, no. 1 (1986): 31-52.

LEASKA, MITCHELL ALEXANDER. *Virginia Woolf's* LIGHTHOUSE: *A Study in Critical Method*. New York: Columbia University Press, 1970.

RUDDICK, LISA COLE. *The Seen and the Unseen: Virginia Woolf's* TO THE LIGHTHOUSE. Cambridge, Massachusetts: Harvard University Press, 1977.

VOGLER, THOMAS A., ed. *Twentieth-Century Interpretations of* TO THE LIGHTHOUSE: *A Collection of Critical Essays*. Englewood Cliffs, New Jersey: Prentice-Hall, 1970.

REVIEW & RESOURCES

A NOTE ON THE TYPE

The typeface used in SparkNotes study guides is Sabon, created by master typographer Jan Tschichold in 1964. Tschichold revolutionized the field of graphic design twice: first with his use of asymmetrical layouts and sanserif type in the 1930s when he was affiliated with the Bauhaus, then by abandoning assymetry and calling for a return to the classic ideals of design. Sabon, his only extant typeface, is emblematic of his latter program: Tschichold's design is a recreation of the types made by Claude Garamond, the great French typographer of the Renaissance, and his contemporary Robert Granjon. Fittingly, it is named for Garamond's apprentice, Jacques Sabon.

SPARKNOTES
TEST PREPARATION
GUIDES

The SparkNotes team figured it was time to cut standardized tests down to size. We've studied the tests for you, so that SparkNotes test prep guides are:

Smarter
Packed with critical-thinking skills and test-
  taking strategies that will improve your score.

Better
Fully up to date, covering all new features of the tests,
  with study tips on every type of question.

Faster
Our books cover exactly what you need to
  know for the test. No more, no less.

SparkNotes Guide to the SAT & PSAT
SparkNotes Guide to the SAT & PSAT — Deluxe Internet Edition
SparkNotes Guide to the ACT
SparkNotes Guide to the ACT — Deluxe Internet Edition
SparkNotes SAT Verbal Workbook
SparkNotes SAT Math Workbook
SparkNotes Guide to the SAT II Writing
5 More Practice Tests for the SAT II Writing
SparkNotes Guide to the SAT II U.S. History
5 More Practice Tests for the SAT II History
SparkNotes Guide to the SAT II Math Ic
5 More Practice Tests for the SAT II Math Ic
SparkNotes Guide to the SAT II Math IIc
5 More Practice Tests for the SAT II Math IIc
SparkNotes Guide to the SAT II Biology
5 More Practice Tests for the SAT II Biology
SparkNotes Guide to the SAT II Physics

SPARKNOTES™ LITERATURE GUIDES

1984

The Adventures of
  Huckleberry Finn

The Adventures of Tom
  Sawyer

The Aeneid

All Quiet on the
  Western Front

And Then There Were
  None

Angela's Ashes

Animal Farm

Anna Karenina

Anne of Green Gables

Anthem

Antony and Cleopatra

Aristotle's Ethics

As I Lay Dying

As You Like It

Atlas Shrugged

The Awakening

The Autobiography of
  Malcolm X

The Bean Trees

The Bell Jar

Beloved

Beowulf

Billy Budd

Black Boy

Bless Me, Ultima

The Bluest Eye

Brave New World

The Brothers
  Karamazov

The Call of the Wild

Candide

The Canterbury Tales

Catch-22

The Catcher in the Rye

The Chocolate War

The Chosen

Cold Mountain

Cold Sassy Tree

The Color Purple

The Count of Monte
  Cristo

Crime and Punishment

The Crucible

Cry, the Beloved
  Country

Cyrano de Bergerac

David Copperfield

Death of a Salesman

The Death of Socrates

The Diary of a Young
  Girl

A Doll's House

Don Quixote

Dr. Faustus

Dr. Jekyll and Mr. Hyde

Dracula

Dune

East of Eden

Edith Hamilton's
  Mythology

Emma

Ethan Frome

Fahrenheit 451

Fallen Angels

A Farewell to Arms

Farewell to Manzanar

Flowers for Algernon

For Whom the Bell
  Tolls

The Fountainhead

Frankenstein

The Giver

The Glass Menagerie

Gone With the Wind

The Good Earth

The Grapes of Wrath

Great Expectations

The Great Gatsby

Greek Classics

Grendel

Gulliver's Travels

Hamlet

The Handmaid's Tale

Hard Times

Harry Potter and the
  Sorcerer's Stone

Heart of Darkness

Henry IV, Part I

Henry V

Hiroshima

The Hobbit

The House of Seven
  Gables

I Know Why the Caged
  Bird Sings

The Iliad

Inferno

Inherit the Wind

Invisible Man

Jane Eyre

Johnny Tremain

The Joy Luck Club

Julius Caesar

The Jungle

The Killer Angels

King Lear

The Last of the
  Mohicans

Les Miserables

A Lesson Before Dying

The Little Prince

Little Women

Lord of the Flies

The Lord of the Rings

Macbeth

Madame Bovary

A Man for All Seasons

The Mayor of
  Casterbridge

The Merchant of Venice

A Midsummer Night's
  Dream

Moby Dick

Much Ado About
  Nothing

My Antonia

Narrative of the Life of
  Frederick Douglass

Native Son

The New Testament

Night

Notes from
  Underground

The Odyssey

The Oedipus Plays

Of Mice and Men

The Old Man and the
  Sea

The Old Testament

Oliver Twist

The Once and Future
  King

One Day in the Life of
  Ivan Denisovich

One Flew Over the
  Cuckoo's Nest

One Hundred Years of
  Solitude

Othello

Our Town

The Outsiders

Paradise Lost

A Passage to India

The Pearl

The Picture of Dorian
  Gray

Poe's Short Stories

A Portrait of the Artist
  as a Young Man

Pride and Prejudice

The Prince

A Raisin in the Sun

The Red Badge of
  Courage

The Republic

Richard III

Robinson Crusoe

Romeo and Juliet

The Scarlet Letter

A Separate Peace

Silas Marner

Sir Gawain and the
  Green Knight

Slaughterhouse-Five

Snow Falling on Cedars

Song of Solomon

The Sound and the Fury

Steppenwolf

The Stranger

Streetcar Named
  Desire

The Sun Also Rises

A Tale of Two Cities

The Taming of the
  Shrew

The Tempest

Tess of the d'Urbervilles

Their Eyes Were
  Watching God

Things Fall Apart

The Things They
  Carried

To Kill a Mockingbird

To the Lighthouse

Treasure Island

Twelfth Night

Ulysses

Uncle Tom's Cabin

Walden

War and Peace

Wuthering Heights

A Yellow Raft in Blue
  Water